Wahlstrom in Selber (p 133)
shifts/lessons for earlier liminal ages:
- au
- ide
- community
- dev. of Robust & reasoned
  discourse
how play out in
~~similar~~ to Gurak's book?

Persuasion and Privacy in Cyberspace

Laura J. Gurak

Persuasion and Privacy
in Cyberspace

The Online Protests over Lotus MarketPlace

and the Clipper Chip

Yale University Press   New Haven and London

Designed by Sonia L. Scanlon.
Set in Bodoni type by Tseng Information
Systems, Durham, North Carolina.
Printed in the United States of America by
BookCrafters, Inc., Chelsea, Michigan.

Gurak, Laura J.
Persuasion and privacy in cyberspace : the
online protests over Lotus MarketPlace and
the Clipper Chip / Laura J. Gurak.
p.   cm.
Includes bibliographical references and
index.
ISBN 0-300-06963-4 (alk. paper)
1. Information superhighway.   2. Internet
(Computer network)   3. Internet (Computer
network)—Social aspects.   I. Title.
HE7568.G87   1997
302.23—dc20   96-38472
CIP

A catalogue record for this book is available
from the British Library.

The paper in this book meets the guidelines
for permanence and durability of the
Committee on Production Guidelines for
Book Longevity of the Council on Library
Resources.

10   9   8   7   6   5   4   3   2   1

This book is dedicated to the interdisciplinarians among us who seek to blend humanistic concerns with technological development by asking hard questions, challenging deterministic attitudes, and working to make our technologies usable, understandable, fair, and accessible.

seems to be all that Wahlstrom called for —

↳ tho doesn't mention ethics, good citizens, or moral obligat

CONTENTS

    Speculation and soothsaying run rampant concerning any new technology, but the latest round of discussion regarding the future status of life in, on, and with the Internet comes close to breaking records not only for its sheer volume but also for its intensity of speculation. Technoprophets and forecasters from all disciplines and backgrounds have been rushing forth to help us answer these questions of our time: What is the shape of coming computerized communication technology? What will the social spaces and rhetorical forums of the future look like? What is the information superhighway, and how will it change our social, educational, and political connections? These are compelling questions, because communicating over the Internet is indeed revolutionary and—as did the railroad, telephone, radio, and television—brings with it the potential for much change in how we perceive distance, time, space, and global boundaries. Yet it is important to move away from generalizations about life in cyberspace and begin to analyze specific instances of computer-mediated communication, not only as a way of understanding patterns of current discourse but also as a method of building theory so we can design communication systems that encourage new social spaces that are appropriate, functional, accessible, and, perhaps, even democratic.

    As a case study of life on the Internet at the end of the twentieth century, this book has two primary purposes. First, it looks at persuasion in terms of rhetorical theory (as distinguished from persuasion theory) and brings two powerful concepts from this body of theory—ethos and delivery—into the public arena by using these concepts to explain actions on the Internet. Although popular conceptions of the word *rhetoric* focus only on what Plato thought of as "bad rhetoric" (rooted in the verbal wordplay of the sophists, who could prove any point regardless of truth), rhetorical theory also provides a critical lens through which one can view and under-

Wahlstrom / ethical action

stand contemporary social phenomena. Along with this function as a critical tool, rhetoric is and has always been a heuristic, a tool for creating discourse and making action; for Aristotle, who canonized the first theory of rhetoric, rhetoric was the "art of finding in any given case the available means of persuasion." Thus, in this book I illustrate that by understanding the rhetorical dynamics, specifically ethos and delivery, in relation to discourse in the online social spaces of the Internet, we can find common language not only to critique this discourse but also to build communication systems that allow for a range of possibilities. While performing this rhetorical analysis and looking at ethos and delivery in online social actions, this book provides a discussion about computer technology, society, and the not-too-distant future. The stories of Lotus MarketPlace and the Clipper chip provide numerous visions of communication and, more broadly, social and political life in cyberspace. The protests over MarketPlace and Clipper were not about the flavor of a soft drink or the price of a new car; these social actions took place *using* computer technology, and they were at the same time *about* computer technology itself and about the competing visions of how we can and should use such technology in the future.

Roadmap

method

Because of its dual purpose (language criticism and speculation about privacy and the Internet), this book has been written with a broad audience in mind. At the center of this audience are those scholars who are interested in the relation of language and technology, along with researchers in computer-mediated communication from the many disciplines that compose this new field of study: computer science, sociology, history of technology, public policy, psychology, management, and technical communication. This book is also intended for anyone interested in computer privacy and social aspects of computing and in the various ways we might shape the online social spaces of the future.

② Another, albeit secondary, purpose of this book is the desire to document the two cases of Lotus MarketPlace and the Clipper chip, as they represent the earliest uses of the Internet for social action. Such documentation of rhetorical discourse on the Internet, because discourse in cyberspace moves quickly, is difficult if not impossible to trace, and is often not maintained in archives. Conversation in cyberspace essentially disappears when email files are deleted and electronic lists are purged from host computers. Yet any attempt to "document" a social action naturally raises issues of objectivity. Most historians have long recognized that it is impossible to tell a story without a point of view; therefore, although I offer the stories of Lotus MarketPlace and the Clipper chip with as much detail as possible (so readers can, while viewing these cases through my eyes, come to their own conclusions), it is ultimately my reading of these cases that takes place on the pages of this book. Still, it is my hope that this reading will not only provide a critical analysis of these two cases but also supply future researchers and policy makers with documentation of these early online social actions.

Because of the multiple purposes and broad audience of this book, I have attempted to strike a balance between the amount of theory presented and the cases themselves. To this end, after a discussion in Chapter 1, I have relegated much of the detailed theoretical discussions to the endnotes in hopes of making this book accessible to a wide audience and keeping the compelling stories of Lotus and Clipper in the foreground. This approach may leave some rhetorical theorists wishing for more subtle discussions of theory, specifically the notion that ethos and delivery (often considered solely classical concepts) are the most significant rhetorical dynamics in online discourse. Yet I strongly believe that the lessons to be learned from the MarketPlace and Clipper protests are most usefully conveyed to a wide audience; furthermore, the dynamics of ethos and delivery explicated in this book should be viewed as a starting point for other theorists who wish to examine the rhetorical dynamics of communication in cyberspace. Certainly, a broad range of outlooks in both classical and contemporary rhetorical theory as well as other disciplinary perspectives will be useful in examining communication in the new forum of cyberspace, and it is my hope that this book will inspire others to continue this effort.

theory body / for case studies

It is only by building on individual case studies that we can create a base of understanding from which to design communication systems of the future.

This book is one of the first to deal with the still-novel and rather complex issue of how to treat research material taken from the Internet. Although it is easy to find a model for the use of certain Internet material, such as online newsletters or magazines, it is less clear how to think about individual postings to electronic newsgroups and listserv mailing lists. One option is to view them as conversation, while the other is to consider them published material.

In this book, I have treated material from a publicly accessible electronic forum as published material and have cited quotations from such texts in the endnotes. All idiosyncrasies of spelling, punctuation, and grammar have been preserved unless otherwise noted. Yet even though my use of this material is criticism and thus would no doubt fall under the fair use provisions for purposes of copyright, I have made one significant change: I have not used real names of the authors of these Internet postings. Instead, except in cases where I obtained explicit permission or where the person is a public figure (including a list moderator), I have used pseudonyms, indicated by the use of square brackets within the texts themselves and the use of quotation marks in the footnoted citations. Thus, I have cited Internet postings with accuracy and with respect for privacy balanced by a belief that material posted to publicly accessible Internet forums can and should be used by scholars and researchers. The Appendix contains a more detailed description of the methodological concerns of using Internet texts as research data.

ACKNOWLEDGMENTS

I wish to thank the many colleagues and associates who have given me advice and support during the creation of this book, beginning with James Zappen, Teresa Harrison, Deborah Johnson, and S. Michael Halloran of Rensselaer Polytechnic Institute, and Carolyn Miller of North Carolina State University. Many thanks go to Marc Rotenberg of the Electronic Privacy Information Center (EPIC), who, while affiliated with Computer Professionals for Social Responsibility (CPSR), gave me complete access to a wealth of documents during my early research on Lotus MarketPlace and who over the years has been a valuable and supportive professional associate. In addition, thanks to Mary Culnan of Georgetown University for her assistance during the early stage of my research on the MarketPlace case.

I should like to thank my supportive and encouraging colleagues at the University of Minnesota, including Billie Wahlstrom, for our discussions about rhetoric, technology, and human communication. Thanks also to Alan Gross for his advice and support during the entire book-writing process, and for his insights into how classical concepts lend themselves to contemporary discourse. Thanks also to Ann Duin, Mary Lay, Art Walzer, and my other colleagues in the rhetoric department for their consideration and support. In addition, I thank my colleague and friend Josephine Lee for her friendship and encouragement during this process.

For her excellent research assistance on the Clipper case, her continued eye on "net happenings," and her editorial and mechanical assistance with the final drafts of the manuscript, I thank my research assistant, Christine Silker. In addition, portions of this book were researched and written with the support of research funds from the Graduate School of the University of Minnesota. I am grateful for this support.

I should like to thank Jean Thomson Black, my editor at Yale

Acknowledgments

University Press, for her vision and assistance in helping me turn these two stories into a book that is accessible outside of the narrow confines of my own academic discipline. Thanks also to Jenya Weinreb of Yale University Press for her careful and incisive editing.

Thank you to my parents, Carl and Eileen Gurak, for all their support. Sadly, my father did not live to see the completion of this book, which would have pleased him greatly, both because he had come to enjoy using the Internet during his last years of life and because he was a great supporter and friend.

Finally, thank you to my partner and intellectual colleague Nancy Bayer for her patience and support, and for her encouragement and friendship during the evolution of this book.

Persuasion and Privacy in Cyberspace

1 Introduction: *Persuasion, Community, and Cyberspace*

In the spring of 1990, Lotus Development Corporation announced a product called MarketPlace: Households. MarketPlace was to be a direct-mail marketing database for personal computers that would contain the names, addresses, and spending habits of 120 million American consumers. After MarketPlace was announced, computer privacy advocates became concerned that the product could be an invasion of privacy and even a potential danger (some were concerned about possibilities of targeting specific individuals for robbery, for example). Debates, discussions, and online petitions concerning MarketPlace quickly filled the Internet. In what was the first such action in cyberspace,[1] MarketPlace was quickly defeated: more than thirty thousand people contacted Lotus and asked that their names be removed from the database. The product was never released, and the results were hailed by some as a "victory for computer populism" (Winner 1991).

A few years later, in 1993, the Clinton administration announced a proposed federal standard for encryption known as Clipper. The controversy surrounding the Clipper chip involved the government's proposed ownership of the encryption algorithm, or key, for decoding information. Advocates for privacy and free speech, alarmed at this specter of Big Brother, organized online discussions, newsgroups, and an Internet-based petition drive. The Internet again became the site of debate and action. As in the Lotus case, a community of privacy advocates used the Internet to disseminate technical information and organize those concerned with privacy and technology.

This book tells the stories of these two online protests, which dealt with computers, privacy, and the shape of communication technology and society in the twenty-first century. The people involved in these protests used a variation of the very technology they were concerned with in order to interact and disseminate information about MarketPlace and Clipper. Those who worried that Lotus MarketPlace would spread their names and personal information across the country were making some of that same information available to wide numbers of computer users when they sent email messages about the product across the Internet. And many Clipper protesters who regularly spoke of Big Brother were software developers and cryptographers who designed encryption software; some of the participants in the online Clipper debate regularly used encryption in their online transactions. One reason both these online actions were so far reaching and in large part successful is that the people doing the protesting understood the technology well enough to be cautious about it and, furthermore, actually to use it to raise awareness.

Yet in each case, protesters and online discussants believed that certain fundamental differences existed between their use and vision of computer technology and cyberspace and the vision held by such large entities as Lotus (at that time a major software developer) and the federal government. Although participants in the Lotus protest often sent their names and addresses out across the Internet, these people *chose* the type and amount of personal information that was circulated, as well as the distribution method. Similarly, anti-Clipper activists used computer technology and made decisions about encryption based on choice, not government mandate. These competing visions about personal privacy, choice, and control in cyberspace are at the heart of what is taking place in, on, and around the Internet at the end of the twentieth century, as we shift from an industrial society to what has been characterized as an information society.

The Internet, originally designed by the Department of Defense to allow scientists and engineers to communicate and share research data, quickly expanded and became an important tool for universities and major research institutions. The acceptance and affordability of personal computers, an increasing number of commercial online services, and a president and vice president whose

[handwritten margin notes: "didn't survive."; "now regular columns devoted to it — even in the funnies""]

platforms included plans for an "information superhighway" have made such terms as *the net, flaming,* and *the Web* almost household words. In every major paper across the United States, a story about the Internet appears almost daily, and new system software facilitates access to the Internet. But while the capability to connect is being promoted widely, the policy issues are often left up for grabs, with many differing visions of life in cyberspace being offered at every turn.

[handwritten margin note: "of. growing quicker than policies (who?)"]

The debates about Lotus MarketPlace and the Clipper chip took place on a level well beyond that of the individual concerns raised in each action. Competing visions of society's future in the online world offer dichotomous scenarios. On the one hand are the cautionary tales of the new information technology as a potential danger, which threatens a "loss of tens of millions of jobs in the years ahead" (Rifkin 1995, 33) and brings with it the potential to "isolate us from one another and cheapen the meaning of actual experience" (Stoll 1995, 3). On the other hand are the technological optimists, who see great possibilities for community and humanity —possibilities for "drawing people into greater world harmony" (Negroponte 1995, 230) and creating orderly, efficient, and fun electronic worlds with few negative side effects (Gates, Myhnold, and Rinearson 1995).

[handwritten margin notes: "dangers"; "pluses"]

Such bipolar forecasting about the technological future is certainly not new; both views about computers and society were expressed at the very beginning of computer technology. Joseph Weizenbaum's 1976 work, for example, outlined the potential dangers of using computers as models of human thought because such thinking could easily strengthen our already strong rationalist outlook on society. At the same time, however, people in the fields of business, science, and engineering were excited about the potential for creating a highly efficient world enhanced by these new machines.

Within the context of such dichotomous positions, how can we critically analyze the possible social and humanistic outcomes of life in cyberspace? In most cases, the problems and potentials of any new technology are far more complex than either the doomsayers or the optimists acknowledge. Many proponents of these positions rely on overgeneralizations and do not look at specific cases. From a completely different perspective, however, is the ongoing research in an area that has come to be known as computer-mediated communication (CMC), an effort to study the interpersonal, social, and organizational aspects of online communication. Starr Roxanne Hiltz and Murray Turoff's book *The Network Nation*, first published in 1978 and reprinted in 1993, is one of the earliest studies of online communication. Their work, along with that of Lee Sproull and Sara Kiesler (1986) and others, raises significant questions about the specific social interactions in cyberspace. Both bodies of work, for example, note that the lack of social cues and easy anonymity of CMC may account for the increase of hostile behavior ("flaming") often seen online. Research in CMC continues in the social sciences and humanities (Herring 1993; Lea et al. 1992; Rice and Love 1987), especially since the current interest in the Internet.[2]

But while the "doom or glory" positions about cyberspace are often overly simplistic or generalized, the research positions sometimes take too close a look, relying on experimental-style research methods to study small groups of computer users on limited computer networks. These studies have provided many insightful conclusions about online communication, but as some have pointed out (Lea et al. 1992), they often do not account for the context of the interaction and therefore may not be relevant outside their specific subject pool and experimental setting. Furthermore, until recently, these studies have favored the position that computer-mediated communication has the potential to act as the great equalizer in terms of status, decision making, and individual power—a position that is beginning to be called into question (Spears and Lea 1994).

In this book, therefore, I make a place between the sweeping and dichotomous yet interesting stories of the technological forecasters on the one hand and the somewhat narrow but more rigorous social science experiments in CMC on the other. I do this by providing an empirical analysis of life on the Internet that has real evidence to support its claims but that is broader than a discrete experiment because of its use of rhetorical criticism, an approach which has traditionally been highly empirical (Halloran 1984) but which retains the critical and somewhat broad lens of a narrative or literary critic. By analyzing the Lotus and Clipper protests from a rhetorical perspective, I offer insight into what made these online protests function and into what the competing visions of the Internet presented by these stories suggest more generally. At its highest and somewhat implicit level, this book argues that these two cases illustrate the actions of online communities. At a more specific level, this book maintains that the Lotus and Clipper communities exemplified a new kind of rhetorical entity: they were communities whose use of language was focused around social action, or what rhetorician Kenneth Burke (1969) would call the "use of language as a symbolic means of inducing cooperation" (43), but whose use of this language took place in a new social space, a virtual place of incredible speed and reach. I argue that two rhetorical features, community ethos and the novel mode of delivery on computer networks, are critical to rhetorical online communities because these features sustain the community and its motive for action in the absence of physical commonality or traditional face-to-face methods of establishing presence and delivering a message. The features of ethos and delivery are not new in the public-speaking arena; both have been important since the early Greek rhetorics of Plato and Aristotle. But online, ethos and delivery take on new significance.

At issue on one level, therefore, is how traditional rhetorical activities, such as speeches or public debates, conducted in the new online spaces differ or are enhanced or problematized because of the uses of computer-mediated communication technologies. Rhetorical discourse, for example, has until recently functioned primarily in the world of physicality. A rhetor's ability to reach out to an audience has traditionally been directly linked to his or her presence in a physical setting, with credibility established through one's persona, or ethos, and one's ability to deliver physically an effective speech or message. Communication technologies, however, beginning with the printed page but especially evident with electronic technologies, have shifted the focus of traditional

rhetorical activities away from physical location, allowing participants to "break the bonds of proximate communication" through
communication technologies that feature "asynchronicity," where
"distance issues" of time and space do not limit the formation of
communities (Kaufer and Carley 1994, 33–35). Within these new
online communities, the rhetorical features of delivery and ethos
are still critical, but in slightly altered ways.

In providing a rhetorical analysis of the Lotus and Clipper chip
online protests, this book illustrates how delivery and ethos function within the online communities that are debating the many
future visions of cyberspace. These features are powerful, but this
power to form specialized communities with such great speed may
also bring with it problems of exclusion, introversion, and inaccurate information. As our global village grows ever more accessible
because of technology but also ever more complex because of the
diversity of its inhabitants, the rhetorical dynamics of delivery and
ethos in cyberspace during the Lotus and Clipper debates help
illustrate the complexities of communication in the online forum.

The Lotus and Clipper cases have many similarities but also
some fundamental differences, and in light of the current competing visions of the Internet, they make for an informative and
challenging contrastive analysis. Both are examples of online social
action; the protest over Lotus MarketPlace was arguably the first
such action in cyberspace. Furthermore, both protests involved
a fundamental concern with who owns and controls information
and who can and should have the power to use this information.
And from a rhetorical perspective, both cases involved the power
of electronic delivery and the appeal of community ethos to support a cause and effectively circulate information. But in a sense,
these cases suggest two somewhat different visions of cyberspace.
The Lotus protest was a bottom-up structure. Although Computer
Professionals for Social Responsibility (CPSR) was involved in the
early advocacy work, it was a form letter from an individual pro-
tester that became the most highly circulated piece of email. This
letter and a few other notes from individuals were posted and reposted by people across the network; it was this process that made

these messages so popular. In contrast, the most significant electronic message in the Clipper protest was an online petition, organized and maintained by CPSR. Although this petition was subject to the same reposting process, it was structured from the top down *Clipper* by an organized advocacy group.

What these cases suggest, then, is that the rhetorical dynamics of delivery and ethos are powerful, but that the ultimate uses of these and all rhetorical skills in online communication technology are governed not by some determined set of technological forces but rather by human agency. *agency* The organizational model we choose to apply to the design and use of this technology will bring with it certain social implications. Bottom-up structure and complete freedom of speech creates one sort of system; top-down structure and gatekeeping creates another. The technological forecasters would have us believe that the future has already happened and is simply waiting for us to reach it. Yet such case studies as Lotus and Clipper suggest that what shape the future social spaces will assume is our choice, and that an understanding of rhetoric *balance* and language as a social force may help us construct systems that *soc. constr.* strike a balance between complete anarchy and complete control. *partic.*

soc. respons.
indiv. respons.

Community from Physical to Virtual

In ancient Greece, where Western rhetorical theory was first codified, debate often took place in the common gathering place of the polis, where citizens engaged in public debate and exchanged ideas. This centrality of *place* in rhetorical discourse has remained with us until recently in the form of town meetings, often held in central public halls. In contemporary society, however, with its diverse communities of interest dispersed over vast distances, the central town meeting place is no longer a viable option. Yet communication technologies provide a potential means to span the physical boundaries of local communities and, as Barber (1984, 275) and others have suggested, provide potential forums for citizen participation. Telephone, radio, television, and, most recently, computer-mediated communication are some of the technologies providing new shapes for the forums where public debate takes place, and the Lotus and Clipper protests are two of the earliest instances of the use of CMC for social action.

Key to understanding what happened in these online protests is the concept of community. The protests functioned as they did because people across cyberspace worked as a new kind of community, similar in some features to traditional communities but unique in its manifestation in the virtual world. As in traditional communities, network participants were located in the same "place." Instead of a physical forum, however, this place was a new kind of public space, an electronic and virtual place of such speed and simultaneity that people with common values quickly gathered around the issue and took action. As in many communities, participants in both protests were linked by common values; yet in the cyberforum, these links were not limited by physical distance or time. Participants moved easily from place to place, forming and reforming communities with a fluid and dynamic quality. Although many network participants and observers casually use the term *community* to describe what happens when groups of people come together in the virtual forums of cyberspace, in this book I suggest a more thorough and carefully articulated sense of community in relation to the cyberspace forum.

The term *community* has traditionally been used in a physical sense, evoking the idea of neighborhood or place. Performing civic duties for one's community, for example, often means working in the local neighborhood for the benefit of the other members of the neighborhood. As Dennis Poplin (1972) indicates, the notion of community has traditionally been used "to refer to such units of social and territorial organization as hamlets, villages, towns, cities, and metropolitan villages," thus invoking the sense of "community as place" (9–10). Anthony Cohen (1985) also notes that traditional sociological studies of community have examined groups of people who reside in the same physical place.

Yet the concept of community is rooted in both physicality or place *and* common values or cultural habits. Many have looked to sociologist Ferdinand Toennies's concept of *gemeinschaft* as the basis of defining community (Barber 1984; Morgan 1942; Walls 1993). Toennies distinguishes between *gesellschaft*, or society, and *gemeinschaft*, or community. Gesellschaft, he argues, is based on laws and other formal relations, while gemeinschaft is the more spontaneous relationships that develop based on physicality *and* customs and values. Jan Walls (1993), in her attempt to clarify the concept of community in relation to the development of global computer networks, describes gemeinschaft as a "natural group-ing of people based on kinship and neighborhood, shared culture, and folkways" (154). Thus, along with the physical nearness of place, communities also require the common attributes of shared culture, or what Cohen (1985) calls a "common body of symbols" used by the community members to make meaning and sustain the sense of community (16). When Cohen suggests that what is important about these shared symbols is the "meanings imputed to them by their members" (40), he points out that values and cul-tural connotations are central in understanding community.

Similarly, the concept of interpretive community, which can be traced in part to Stanley Fish (Harris 1989), focuses less on physi-cal location than on values and culture. It is not one's neighbor-hood but rather one's way of seeing the world that identifies and defines interpretive communities. Although members of an inter-pretive community may share some physical space for a period of time, an interpretive community, says Joseph Harris, "refers not so much to specific physical groupings of people as to a kind of loose dispersed network of individuals who share certain habits of mind" (14). In both the interpretive community and its theoretical offspring known to composition scholars as the "discourse commu-nity," [3] the notion "loses its rooting in a particular place" so that "in the place of physical nearness we are given like-mindedness" (15). This sense of community has subsequently been demonstrated by those interested in the values of specific groupings of professionals. Thomas Kuhn's (1970) notion of scientific communities, for ex-ample, is based on the idea of its members sharing common values and cultural norms. In the political arena as well, the idea of community is one rooted in its members' sense of values and purpose (Laclau 1991; Mouffe 1991).

These two general ideas of community, physicality and shared values, provide the basis of many network observers' sense of the "electronic community." Network participants often describe cyberspace as a place, choosing such verbs as *go* to indicate moving between conferences, or using other language that normally indicates a physical setting. In the following excerpt from the Lotus postings, the speaker sounds as if he is standing in a room filled with people:

> i've been reading over everyone's shoulder here and
> have a couple of naive oberservations.[4]

Researchers have also observed this physicality of cyberspace, calling it a "virtual landscape" (Selfe and Selfe 1996), a "conceptual space where words, human relationships . . . are manifested by people using CMC technology" (Rheingold 1993b, 5), or a "social space where people connect with one another" (Harasim 1993, 15). Some CMC technologies, such as MUDs (multi-user dimensions) and MOOs (MUDs object oriented), which are increasingly being used beyond their original design for game playing, are constructed around the metaphor of rooms, offices, and other physical locations.[5] This sense of cyberforum as place is evident in both the Lotus and Clipper cases, not only in the language of place used by participants but also in the dynamics of the discourse. Participants often spoke and interacted as if in they were in the same room. Within these electronic spaces and places, cyberspace participants moved among forums that attract and connect people with common values, needs, and interests, recalling Allucquere Rosanne Stone's (1992) description of the earliest cyberspaces as "virtual communities, passage points for collections of common beliefs and practices that united people who were physically separated" (85). These observations confirm the prediction of J. R. C. Licklider and others (designers of the original ARPANET, precursor to the Internet) who in 1968 suggested that "on-line interactive communities" of the future would be "communities not of common location, but of *common interest*" (30). Furthermore, as participants on computer networks interact with each other, they begin to learn the tacit rules and understandings of the network communities, illustrating Cohen's (1985) point that "community . . . is where one acquires 'culture' " (15).[6]

Yet unlike traditional communities, electronic communities allow people to "lurk" (without being seen) outside the culture, reading yet not participating, and deciding if a particular discussion is of interest. If not, they can move on and find another location. Furthermore, people can fine-tune their selections and go directly to the community that best fits their needs. Online spaces are extremely specialized; thousands of Internet-based discussion groups, known as Usenet newsgroups, currently exist to discuss subjects ranging from skiing to particle physics to computer software to beer brewing. After connecting to and observing any of these online social spaces, people can leave, come back, join another community, and so on. Any sense of fixedness or rigidity is replaced by a fluid and open feeling; the technology allows and seems to encourage such types of community. So while network participants often feel that they and others are, as one computer forum participant put it, "member[s] of the Internet community,"[7] they also feel, and are, part of many other subcommunities.

In both the Lotus and Clipper cases, participants debated and protested by moving among many virtual places of common interest: Usenet newsgroups, electronic conferences and forums, electronic mail connections, and company bulletin boards. They shared a concern about personal privacy, specifically computer privacy and the use of the Internet, and they spoke to each other with a sense of common purpose and values. They displayed a common culture through their use of language and special symbols. Furthermore, they were engaged in purposeful social action in a public arena, which suggests another aspect to their community. This final quality of community, one that has only recently received attention from scholars, is the idea of these communities as persuasive, or *rhetorical,* bodies.

The Rhetorical Dynamics of an Electronic Community

Carolyn Miller (1993) argues that "rhetoric should take seriously its social grounding by exploring and using the concept of community more fully and more critically" (80). Exploring the connections between rhetorical action and political community, she suggests that a focus on the community-based nature of rhetoric will provide a framework for discourse in contemporary society, where diverse communities "coexist and overlap each other" (91). But where does one begin exploring the dynamics of these communities in order to build such a framework? It makes sense to start this endeavor by turning to and analyzing individual cases that highlight community action of a rhetorical nature.

Both the Lotus MarketPlace and Clipper cases provide excellent examples of rhetorical community, here with an emphasis on the electronic forum. In the Lotus case, this virtual community looked like the electronic community just described: a group with common values and culture located in the space of an electronic forum. Yet it was also a community with a rhetorical intent toward purposeful action: to debate and protest in a public arena, to make change, and to bring about action. Therefore, it becomes critical to ask about the specific rhetorical nature of this community with regard to achieving social action. A close look at both online actions shows that they functioned through two rhetorical elements: the appeal of ethos and the canon of delivery, which, I argue, constituted the *dynamics* of the community protest in cyberspace.

Like many communities, the privacy-focused cybercommunity appeared to function through a set of common values and goals. Based on the participants' comments and email addresses, it can be concluded that many (though not all) of the participants were computer scientists or other professionals, often with specialized knowledge and tacit understandings about computer privacy. The way these values were expressed is evident in what in rhetorical terms can be called the ethos of the discourse. In each case, protest postings reflect a certain group ethos: in the Lotus case, this ethos was a personal, angry, and antagonistic voice; in the Clipper case, the group ethos was also angry but at times was highly technical as well. In both cases, the group ethos appealed to others of similar persuasion and made it easy to spread the word to others with similar beliefs.

In classical rhetoric, ethos is associated with the credibility and character of the speaker. Ethos is one of the three modes of appeal—*pathos, ethos,* and *logos*—that make up Aristotle's system of invention. For Aristotle, ethos was part of this broader inventional scheme of "finding in any given case the available means of persuasion" (1356a) and required speakers to "find" and assume the appropriate character traits for a given argument (1378a). The notion of ethos was also a part of the Roman rhetorical tradition (Cherry 1988, 255), as exemplified by Quintilian's sense of the rhetor as "a man of good character and courtesy" (Meador 1983, 166) or Cicero's belief that wisdom must be accompanied by eloquence (1.2).⁸ diff classical views

While rooted in classical rhetoric, ethos is also a contemporary concept used widely to describe the character, tenor, or tone of a rhetor. In general discussion, one often hears references to the ethos of a particular public figure or time period. Along with this common usage, the concept has played a continued role throughout the contemporary rhetorical tradition. Burke's (1969) concept of identification, for example, involves a speaker and audience *identifying* in part based on the character of the speaker.⁹ Throughout this book, the notion of ethos is based on this long-standing definition: the values and character of the speaker or speakers expressed in what has been called a "characteristic manner of holding and expressing ideas" (Halloran 1984, 71).

cf Arist + Burke

LG's def here

The focus of ethos, especially in the classical tradition, has primarily been on individual speakers. Yet in both the Lotus and Clipper cases, ethos was also a group quality, one that characterized the collective sense of character and values. This notion of group ethos has been noted by Michael Halloran (1982), who suggests that "the word *ethos* has both an individual and a collective meaning. It makes sense to speak of the *ethos* of this or that person, but it makes equally good sense to speak of the *ethos* of a particular type of person, of a professional group, or a culture, or an era in history" (62). Furthermore, ethos can be extended to the group persona created by communication technology. In discussing the CMC technology of hypertext, Jay Bolter (1993), noting that "what we mean by the voice of a text was in ancient terms [called] *persona* or *ethos*," suggests the existence of a "hypertextual voice" (107). The ethos of both the Lotus and Clipper cases thus highlights the claim that "*ethos* is not measurable traits displayed by an individual; rather it is a complex set of characteristics constructed by a group, sanctioned by that group, and more readily recognizable to others who belong or share similar values or experiences" (Reynolds 1993, 327).

Although *ethos* is most often used to refer "to the character of an age, era, society, or culture, something like *zeitgeist*" (Reynolds 1993, 327), two additional ways of considering ethos are of special significance to online discourse. The first is the relation of ethos to ethics, a relation that harkens back to the Roman rhetorician Quintilian's definition of a rhetor as a "good man of character and courtesy," or what has also been characterized as "a good man speaking well." In other words, it is not just the projection of the character of a speaker or group, but also his (or her, or the group's) actual moral and ethical character that is relevant to both the effectiveness and the quality of the speech. In online discourse, the ethical character of the speaker is often unchallenged; the sense of trust among some members of the Internet community is often based on a person's stated professional affiliations and subsequent contributions to life on the Internet. Individuals can be accepted as moral and credible even though the many recipients of an Internet message have never met the author or authors of the message and cannot be sure the authors are who they say they are.[10] In addition, pseudonyms, for example, can be used to mask the name of a

speaker, so that often it is the ethos of the *texts*, not the character — *difference*
of the speaker, that does or does not convince others.

Another aspect of ethos comes from the etymology of the Greek word, which, translated carefully, means a "habitual meeting place," thus invoking an "image of people gathering together in a public place, sharing experiences and ideas" (Halloran 1982, 61). Once this notion of ethos as "space, place, or haunt" has been recognized, we can begin to see ethos "as a social act and a product of a community's character" (Reynolds 1993, 327); in other words, we can see that people come to acquire a community ethos by inhabiting a space and learning its unique communicational characteristics. Nowhere could this concept be more obvious than in the specialized newsgroups and other electronic forums on the Internet, where outsiders are regularly "flamed" until they have come to understand and assimilate the community ethos, and where, as both the Lotus and Clipper cases illustrate, community ethos is the basis for what information other online participants will accept and believe.

In the Lotus and Clipper cases, ethos functioned hand-in-hand with the delivery medium of computer-mediated communication. Delivery, the fifth of the five components, or canons, of rhetorical discourse,[11] traditionally included gestures, facial expressions, vocal intonations, and other physical actions involved in giving a speech. The relation between ethos and delivery in rhetorical theory is well noted and obvious: one's perceived credibility and persona are inherently linked to how one delivers a speech.

In electronic discourse, this relation is equally important, but in a somewhat altered and novel fashion; hence Bolter's (1993) suggestion that "electronic writing compels us to reconsider the classical concept of delivery" (97). Certainly since radio and television, and even more significantly in cyberspace, delivery no longer means the oral presentation of a speech; rather, delivery is now bound up in the *medium* of distribution. Delivery in cyberspace means multiple, simultaneous transmissions of messages across great distance and without regard for time. Furthermore, this cyberdelivery allows and even promotes interaction between the original author of a message and other online participants through email, interactive live chat sessions, and bulletin boards or Usenet newsgroups. Where ethos was once conveyed to a room or town square full of people via a speaker's physical gestures, it is now sent across the world, conveyed through ASCII characters, unique signature files, and strong language, to thousands of individuals who can immediately respond. When people of similar interests become attracted to a certain message, such communities as the MarketPlace or Clipper protest groups come into existence.

Rhetorical theory offers little in the way of a theory of delivery.[12] Yet, as Kathleen Welch (1990) has noted, electronic technology "has made the fifth canon of delivery (medium) take on the urgency of simultaneous communication" (26). Furthermore, work by David Kaufer and Kathleen Carley (1993, 1994) provides useful concepts for explaining and describing delivery in cyberspace. In their study of communication at a distance, they note the features of reach, asynchronicity, durability, and multiplicity. These features, along with speed, time, and specificity, are the major components in electronic delivery and provide a language for describing delivery in cyberspace.

In both the Lotus and Clipper cases, community ethos worked in conjunction with a delivery that involved speed, great reach, and specificity. In the Lotus case, less than twenty-four hours after an article about MarketPlace appeared in the *Wall Street Journal*, messages spread throughout cyberspace. These messages sped across computer networks, picking up information as they passed from email account to internal company bulletin board and gathering new community members along the way. Messages continued to be distributed in this fashion throughout the protest. Similarly, in the Clipper case, the CPSR electronic petition was circulated quickly throughout cyberspace; anyone could sign the petition electronically with a few simple keystrokes.

The Promise and Problems of Communities in Cyberspace

The rhetorical dynamics of delivery and ethos in online communities bring with them promise but also potential problems. Perhaps the most obvious promise of communication in cyberspace is the potential to provide space for many more voices than have ever before had access to such a powerful communication medium. Although television's reach is vast, it is not interactive, and most people do not have the power to purchase a television station or buy air time. And call-in radio programs cannot compare with the growing number of Internet newsgroups, chat sessions, and mailing lists. Part of the potential of cyberspace is that delivery is extremely efficient. The speed and reach of one email message sent with a single keystroke are astounding, and its audience is extremely targeted: online participants can reach thousands of other people who are interested in a certain topic. Furthermore, the current Internet structure flattens hierarchies, allowing people to correspond with each other regardless of corporate rank.

Yet these same features bring with them many potential problems. Because they are removed from the face-to-face elements of delivery that have until recently been so critical to speech situations, online participants may be inclined toward "uninhibited behavior," often called flaming.[13] This behavior, along with the highly specialized nature of online communities, may exclude those who do not feel comfortable with the prevailing community ethos. Furthermore, the flattened hierarchies and open forums of the Internet can promote the spread of inaccurate information.

Communication in cyberspace is quickly raising numerous intellectual property issues, among them significant challenges to traditional notions of copyright. The common practice of forwarding entire email messages is technically a violation of copyright (Cavazos and Morin 1994), yet online delivery seems to encourage these kinds of violations, which include not only reposting someone else's electronic text but also typing in and transmitting such proprietary materials as newspaper articles and trade secrets. Although some Internet participants argue that copyright law must eventually change to keep pace with the new technology, this kind of deterministic thinking does not answer the broader philosophical questions. Should all materials on the Internet be considered in the public domain? Should authors' rights take a back seat to free access of information? As of this writing, proposed legislation to address many of these issues is opening up a broad public policy debate among academics, students, publishers, and corporate representatives, as each group articulates its needs and visions of intellectual property in cyberspace.

Finally, there is the issue of who has access to online communities. Some counties in the United States still lack telephone service, and although this will certainly change, what will probably not change in the foreseeable future are the power and class structures in this country and around the world. To some extent, current fears about "information have-nots" are well founded. A personal computer, modem, and access fees are still well out of reach for many people, and even if hardware were available, issues of education and training would need to be addressed. In the near future, communities in cyberspace will no doubt continue to be populated by those who have both the financial and educational ability to participate. These problems, and the promise, of community in cyberspace are apparent in the cases of Lotus MarketPlace and the Clipper chip.

2 The Case of Lotus MarketPlace

On April 10, 1990, Lotus Development Corporation announced a "desktop information product" called Lotus MarketPlace. The product, a CD-ROM direct-mail marketing database, was designed to run on Macintosh personal computers, thus giving small businesses easy and affordable access to direct-mailing lists. The product came in two editions: Lotus MarketPlace: Business and Lotus MarketPlace: Households. The Business edition contained information on 7 million American businesses; the Households edition contained information on 120 million American consumers from 80 million households. Lotus MarketPlace: Households was a joint effort of Lotus and Equifax Credit Corporation, which provided the demographic data for the product.[1]

In the months that followed the announcement, more than thirty thousand people contacted Lotus and asked that their names be removed from the Households database. The product, which had been scheduled to be released during the third quarter of 1990, was never released. On January 23, 1991, Lotus announced that it would cancel MarketPlace: Households owing to, in the company's words, "public concerns and misunderstandings of the product, and the substantial, unexpected costs required to fully address consumer privacy issues." Later, Equifax (1991) issued a press release, announcing its "decision to discontinue sales of direct marketing lists derived from the consumer credit file."

From Lotus's first announcement until months after it canceled the product, discussions about MarketPlace: Households filled newspapers, news and computer magazines, and, of most significance to this story, cyberspace. The Internet and other networks buzzed with debates about the product's implications for personal privacy. People posted the address and phone number of Lotus and Equifax and supplied directions for getting names removed from the database. Some people posted form letters that could be signed by anyone and sent to Lotus. Other messages about MarketPlace were forwarded around the Internet, reposted to other newsgroups, and sent off as email messages. In the end, the corporations and network activists acknowledged the role that the networks played in stopping the release of MarketPlace. And some called the event a new form of computer populism (Winner 1991). How exactly did this event come about?

Lotus and Equifax: Product Development

During the second half of 1988, Lotus and Equifax began discussing the possibility of developing what they called a "desktop marketing product for small business." Lotus would provide the software and technical knowledge; Equifax Marketing Decision Systems (a division of Equifax) would supply the demographic data. During this early phase, the two companies did not have an exact plan for the shape of the product. Rather, they were interested in pursuing the idea of a general marketing tool for small businesses (Baker 1991).

According to Equifax, the group was concerned from the beginning with privacy issues. In his testimony before a special U.S. House subcommittee hearing on public and corporate attitudes on privacy, Equifax Senior Vice President John A. Baker indicated that the group "spent a great deal of time and effort from the very beginning of the development of this product to think through numerous privacy and consumer protection issues so that we could build in appropriate controls" (Baker 1991, 9). In an appendix to this testimony, Equifax noted ways in which the company attempted to deal with privacy concerns from the start of the project. For example, Equifax had already hired privacy expert Alan Westin as a consultant for all their credit services. During the early discussions about MarketPlace, Westin was asked to join an internal task force to consult on privacy issues specifically about the product (11). Equifax and Lotus held eight focus groups made up of a "cross section and representative sample of American consumers" and used some of the consumers' comments in developing the final product. The group also wrote a "privacy protection pamphlet," which it distributed to the media, government officials, and privacy and consumer groups (28). In addition, Lotus claimed that MarketPlace would use a screening process to be sure that only "legitimate businesses" were using the product. Finally, the data was to be encrypted on the discs, thus reducing the chance that someone could simply download the data without having the access code from Lotus.

Yet these efforts to deal with privacy issues were not made explicit to the public. During the online protest, many postings accused Lotus and Equifax of being insensitive and unethical in their approach to personal privacy. Furthermore, even when some of these steps toward privacy protection were discussed online, the general sentiment was that these measures were not sufficient. What exactly were "legitimate businesses"? How could Lotus guarantee that its encryption method could not be cracked?

Although Equifax was part of the development effort, the product was to be marketed and sold by Lotus. The initial press release, which described the product as a "new desktop information product for the Apple Macintosh personal computers that allows any business person to perform sophisticated sales prospecting and market analysis," included the suggested retail price ($695), technical specifications, and comments by Lotus officials on the product's potential uses. "MarketPlace extends our expertise in CD-ROM technology to a broad, new base of users—any business person who needs to be more efficient and productive in finding and keeping customers," stated Jim Manzi, then president and CEO of Lotus. Lotus had also made agreements with a number of other companies to produce peripheral products for MarketPlace: Avery Corporation, for example, was to produce specially designed labels to be used with Lotus MarketPlace (Avery Commercial Products Division 1990).

The Households product used 11 CD-ROM discs ("10 regional, 1 national of affluent households") and Macintosh-style icon-driven software. The product contained the following data on each consumer household: name, address, age range, gender, marital status,

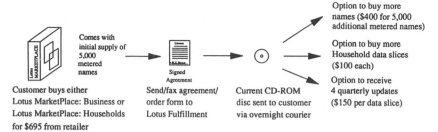

Customer buys either
Lotus MarketPlace: Business or
Lotus MarketPlace: Households
for $695 from retailer

- CD-ROM with Software, Sample Data
- Documentation
- Agreement/Order Form
- Includes purchase of first 5,000 names of
  the user's choice from disc

Figure 2.1. The process by which people who purchased Lotus MarketPlace: Households would obtain direct-mail information from the database. Diagram is based on material in Lotus's original press information kits.

estimated household income, dwelling type, products or lifestyle category (based on previous purchases), and shopping habits. To use MarketPlace, a user would specify a set of parameters. In its press release, Lotus gave the example of a small-business owner who asks for a list of people in the greater Dallas area between the ages of thirty-five and forty-nine, with incomes of more than fifty thousand dollars per year and an "upwardly mobile, success-driven" lifestyle. Once a user made a selection, he or she would be able to view partial information on the screen (names and partial addresses). The user could then buy the full list by calling Lotus and paying for an access code to the encrypted data on the disc. The initial cost of MarketPlace included access to the first five thousand names. Subsequent names could be obtained by calling Lotus and purchasing access to more names.

Lotus MarketPlace was a new approach to direct-mail marketing. Traditionally, mailing lists are maintained on computer databases, either by large specialty mailing organizations (fulfillment centers, mailing houses, or large credit and information companies like Equifax) or by mail-order catalog companies and magazines.

These databases provide an accessible means for making changes or for adding or deleting a customer's record. If, for example, you receive a mailing with your name spelled incorrectly, or if you simply do not wish to receive material from this company, it is simple for the company to locate your record in their database and correct it or delete it. And the Direct Mail Association offers a Mail Preference Service, which allows customers to request that their names be removed from most national mailing lists (Barton 1990, 82).[2]

With Lotus MarketPlace, however, data was provided on CD-ROM. Read Only Memory (ROM) means that data can only be read from the discs; no data can be written to these discs. Therefore, if an individual discovered an error in a mailing generated by the MarketPlace database, this error could not be corrected. He or she would have to write to the Direct Marketing Association and also to Equifax, and then hope that the requested changes were made on the next pressing of MarketPlace discs. This individual would also have to hope that all owners of the Lotus product would buy the updated set of discs.

The Protest

MarketPlace was initially announced in the *New York Times* and other major newspapers and trade journals. The *Times* article, a short piece, simply announced the product and described the basic concept and suggested price. Trade publications focused on features relevant to their audiences. Direct-mail marketing magazines emphasized the potential efficiency of the product; for example, the trade magazine *Direct Marketing* called the product astounding and praised what it would do for direct marketers (Hoke 1990). Computer publications, in contrast, highlighted the interactions of CD-ROM and the Macintosh. Lotus also produced a full-page display advertisement that ran in such business publications as *Fortune* magazine (November 5, 1990, p. 130). This ad pictured rows of men in business suits, some of whom had large bull's-eyes on their backs, and asked, "Wouldn't it be great if new customers were this easy to spot? Now they can be, with Lotus MarketPlace."

It went on to describe how MarketPlace would help "target the customers you want."

Although media reports initially consisted mainly of product announcements, the focus of the coverage soon shifted to privacy concerns. On November 13, 1990, the *Wall Street Journal* published an article entitled "Lotus Product Spurs Fears about Privacy" (Wilke 1990). The *Journal* article discussed the privacy issues raised by MarketPlace and contained interviews with Mary Culnan of Georgetown University, Janlori Goldman of the American Civil Liberties Union, Evan Hendricks of the *Privacy Times*, and Marc Rotenberg of CPSR, all arguing against the product. On the other side of the argument, the article supplied interviews with Dan Schimmel of Lotus, Robert Hilles of Equifax, and Alan Westin, privacy consultant to Equifax. In large part as a response to the *Journal* article, cyberspace discussions about MarketPlace began to heat up in November 1990. Excerpts of the article were sent out across computer privacy newsgroups and discussion lists.

The *Wall Street Journal* article and resulting electronic protests and discussions were based in part on advocacy work begun by CPSR shortly after Lotus announced the MarketPlace product. Early in May 1990, Mary Culnan, a professor at Georgetown University, was working as a volunteer for CPSR's Washington office. She noticed an article about MarketPlace in the "Friday Report," a weekly report by the magazine *Direct Marketing*, and brought the article to the attention of Marc Rotenberg, then the director of the Washington office. On May 16, Rotenberg testified before the House subcommittee. This committee, chaired by Congressman Robert E. Wise, Jr., was set up to investigate the need for a data protection board in the United States. In his testimony, Rotenberg used Lotus MarketPlace as an example of a computer technology with grave implications for personal privacy. He stated that the information contained in MarketPlace "is the most easily accessible collection of personal data on American consumers that has ever been made available in this country" (Rotenberg 1990, 106). CPSR's prepared statement for these hearings, written by Rotenberg, Culnan, and Ronni Rosenberg of Harvard, called Lotus

MarketPlace a "privacy disaster" (Rotenberg 1990, 112). Word spread among privacy advocates. When Mary Culnan spoke before an American Bar Association Panel in early May, Evan Hendricks, editor of the *Privacy Times*, was in the audience, and the *Privacy Times* subsequently ran a story about Lotus MarketPlace in its May 9 edition.

The Washington, D.C., office of CPSR then began developing a plan to research MarketPlace and to make public CPSR's concerns about the privacy implications of the product. During the summer and fall of 1990, CPSR spoke directly with Lotus on more than one occasion. On August 30, representatives from Equifax and Lotus came to Washington and met with Rotenberg and Culnan at the CPSR offices. The meeting, held at the suggestion of Equifax, included a demonstration of the product. During this meeting, Rotenberg questioned the privacy protections taken to prevent identifying individuals within the database (Rotenberg 1993a). In October, Rotenberg corresponded over email with Mitch Kapor, the founder of Lotus and a former Lotus executive who is currently affiliated with the Electronic Frontier Foundation (EFF). Also in October, Rotenberg and another CPSR member corresponded with Dave Reed, chief scientist at Lotus, and debated the privacy implications of the product (Rotenberg 1992). By the time the *Wall Street Journal* article appeared, concern about MarketPlace was in the foreground of the community of computer privacy advocates.

The *Journal* article inspired many of the early postings about MarketPlace. The November 16 electronic issue of RISKS Digest contained three postings about Lotus MarketPlace. The first, dated November 14, summarized two articles from the *Wall Street Journal*, one of which was the article about MarketPlace. A second posting contained excerpts of an unofficial newspaper of Digital Equipment Corporation employees. This posting also summarized the *Journal* article, including pieces of the interviews with Mary Culnan, Marc Rotenberg, and Janlori Goldman. The third posting noted that concerned persons could write to Lotus to have their names removed. Also on November 14, a subdiscussion, or topic, of the Electronic Frontier Foundation conference on the Whole Earth

'Lectronic Link (WELL) network was started with the express purpose of discussing Lotus MarketPlace. Its first posting was also about the *Wall Street Journal* article and contained a small excerpt of the article and some commentary about the process of removing names. Soon, excerpts of the *Journal* article began appearing on other privacy-related online sources, such as the Telecom Privacy Digest.

Quickly, postings moved away from simply informing (citing the *Journal* article, for example) and toward other, more persuasive types of discussions. People began to debate the privacy issues raised by the product and the protest itself, to discuss the product and what it contained, and to make efforts to mobilize. Electronic messages began to echo around the net as people forwarded and reforwarded messages to online conferences and discussion lists.

The most visible note to make its way through cyberspace appeared in late November. Larry Seiler, a New England–based computer professional, was reading news on the Internet and came across a note about MarketPlace. This note contained a summary of the product, some comments about privacy issues and removing names from the database, and the address of Lotus Corporation's Market Name Removal Service (Salz 1993). According to Seiler, he downloaded the note (which he called a "much-forwarded message that had first been sent on November 26"), added his own commentary, and emailed the resulting note to people both inside his company and on the Internet at other organizations. Before long, his message had spread over cyberspace. It was posted to newsgroups, reposted to others, and forwarded on email. Seiler reports that he "very quickly started getting echoes—quite literally, as I received a number of copies back again with long forwarding lists—sometimes entirely inside the company, and sometimes from the outside" (Seiler 1993). The prefaces to many of these reposted messages illustrate the way individuals were forwarding his messages across the world. In one instance, Seiler's note went out as email on the Internet, was passed along as email and posted to various newsgroups, was taken from a newsgroup by someone in British Columbia, was forwarded back to the United States, and was then posted to the WELL. According to a story in *PC Week*, in which Seiler was interviewed, the note "reached computer buffs as far afield as Saudi Arabia" (Fisher 1991b, 156).

The electronic discussions about Lotus MarketPlace, privacy, and the nature of living in an age of electronic information continued through November and December 1990 and into January 1991. A community of computer specialists, academics, and privacy advocates converged in cyberspace to discuss the issue, and some prepared to take action. Because so many of the participants were computer specialists, they understood MarketPlace and were able to make technical arguments about the product. Postings had a range of functions: to inform, to debate the protest, to debate the product, to mobilize, to divulge "secret information," and to discuss other privacy-related issues. One electronic discussion group, devoted entirely to Lotus MarketPlace, contained almost three hundred individual postings.

Lotus Reacts to the Controversy

In all the online debate, Lotus's voice was missing. According to a former Lotus employee who was product manager for the Market-Place group, the company was unfamiliar with the Internet and was thus caught off guard by the power of communication in cyberspace. According to this former employee, Lotus just didn't have a "coordinated strategy to fight the Internet." The MarketPlace development group was not aware of the cyberspace debate until much too late. Even when the group tried to post to the Internet, its lack of familiarity with cyberspace made its efforts ineffective.[3]

Shortly after the publication of the *Wall Street Journal* article, Lotus received a small number of letters that referenced the article and complained about MarketPlace: Households. Given the overall number of readers of the *Journal*, however, company officials did not consider twenty-five letters to be a significant reaction. The MarketPlace group, which was still working on a name-removal process for its product, felt comfortable with the product and with the public's reactions thus far. As one source put it, MarketPlace development team members felt that because of feedback from customer focus groups and other privacy efforts, "things had worked out really well."

Yet Lotus soon began to receive what it noticed were form letters: letters of complaint that had the same basic body of text. These were probably Seiler's letter and others that were distributed on the Internet. Some made reference to receiving the letter "from my friend at [large computer company]." The MarketPlace group wondered how and where these form letters were being distributed. On or around December 18, Lotus received approximately six hundred telephone calls complaining about MarketPlace: Households. The group was shocked, because at that time, according to a former employee, Lotus normally received roughly a thousand phone calls per day for all its products. So six hundred calls concerning just one product, a product not even released, was an unbelievable number. The group began to wonder what had happened.

Once the group had identified the cyberspace discussions as the source of the controversy, the problem became how to respond. The group put together a note, but no one knew where or how to post it. "It was impossible to keep track of where this thing [notes about MarketPlace] was popping up," noted a former employee. Furthermore, no one in the MarketPlace group knew how to access Usenet or post notices. The group eventually asked an engineer at the company about the process of posting an official rebuttal to the online discussions. This message, dated January 3 and posted to the Usenet newsgroup comp.society, acknowledges in its first sentence that the newsgroup had been a forum for discussions about MarketPlace: "In response to recent messages that have appeared here about Lotus. . . ." The posting goes on to provide "some hard facts" that Lotus hoped "will clear up some of the misinformation surrounding the product," and closes with the line "We hope that this clarifies any questions or concerns" (former Lotus employee A 1991).[4]

This businesslike note provoked angry responses from online participants. Along with sending edited copies of Seiler's letter, people were also calling Lotus's toll-free number and sending notes directly to the Internet address of Jim Manzi. A message posted on January 3 to the mailing list tcp-ip, containing the entire Seiler note, had added an additional piece of information, which the author claims to have included "as a community service": Manzi's Internet address.[5] Like the original Seiler note, the note containing Jim Manzi's email address echoed across the Internet.[6] According to one source, Manzi was understandably not happy about getting these notes, and on the day after the New Year's holiday (January 2 or 3), he called a meeting with the MarketPlace project director and said that he wanted the problem of MarketPlace solved.[7]

Just twenty days after Lotus's posting to comp.society, the company announced that it would not release MarketPlace: Households. In a press release, Manzi said that the product was being canceled because, "unfortunately, Lotus MarketPlace: Households is at the apex of an emotional firestorm of public concern about consumer privacy." The media and notes on the Internet indicate that Lotus had received some thirty thousand requests from people who wanted their names removed from the database.[8]

Most of the major newspapers picked up the story the next day, featuring such headlines as "Chalk One Up for Privacy Rights" (Edelman 1991) and "Privacy Flap Kills Lotus Data Base" (O'Connor 1991). The case of Lotus MarketPlace provided a focus over the next few months for many other newspaper and magazine articles to analyze broader issues of computer privacy and direct-mail ethics. A *PC Week* article published in February 1991 talked not only about MarketPlace but also about caller ID technology and about privacy laws (Fisher 1991b). In March, Mary Culnan and John Baker of Equifax wrote a joint column in the *New York Times* where they discussed the failure of MarketPlace.

Throughout cyberspace, word traveled fast. On the same day that Lotus announced the cancellation, notes were posted to all the privacy conferences. The first notes were informational, containing material from a few media sources. A posting on RISKS Digest contained excerpts from the *Wall Street Journal* article of that day and from the Associated Press. Two postings on the WELL announced the cancellation of MarketPlace. One was based on information from Reuters; the other contained a copy of the Lotus press release. The Telecom Digest reposted the story that ran in Compuserve's "Online Today." Along with these informational postings, some notes contained "secret information." On January 24, a note posted to the Telecom Privacy Digest by someone wishing to be anonymous contained what it claimed to be an internal Lotus memo. This memo, dated January 23, was supposedly sent by Lotus executives to its employees. It announces the cancellation of MarketPlace, describes the public's concern with the product, indicates that much of this concern was ill founded, and thanks the employees for their efforts. In the posting of this memo, both the "To:" and "From:" lines are followed by the word "removed" in parentheses. But in another posting of this memo, this time to the WELL on January 28, the "To:" is followed with "All Lotus Employees" and the "From:" with "Jim Manzi." This memo, according to the person posting the note, "has apparently been making the rounds on the net." [9]

"Never Underestimate the Power of the 'Vox Populi' "

Conversations on the net about Lotus MarketPlace quickly tapered off after the product was canceled. Discussions lasted for a few weeks, and in some cases, up until April. Citing a story from the *San Jose Mercury* that commented on the use of the net in the Lotus case, one participant reflected, "Never underestimate the power of the 'vox populi.' " [10] Others had similar comments. The moderator of the Telecom Digest, who had not agreed with the criticisms of MarketPlace, nonetheless wrote:

```
I am *very pleased* to see the way organizations and
institutions are beginning to respect the power of
the net. I've said it before: email, in all it[s]
variations, both as individual correspondence and
as a newsgroup is an extremely potent tool. The
situation with Lotus proves it. Do *not* hesitate
to write letters to people who can make changes in
```

```
things which need changing. Do not hesitate for a
minute to use this net just like newspapers have
been used for years: as a forum—and a powerful one
at that—to get your message across.¹¹
```

Was the Lotus protest a populist action, as political scientist and technology critic Langdon Winner (1991) believed, or was it, as one Lotus executive said, "an epidemic of misinformation and misperception" spread by a specialized group of people on the Internet? This question is worth exploring, because it goes to the heart of one of the claims currently made about network communication: the ability of the Internet to somehow reinvigorate democracy by providing a space for debate and exchange among multiple voices.

Although the specifics of the Lotus MarketPlace protest may not be well remembered today, the fear of what Shoshana Zuboff (1988) described as the "information panopticon" is still all too prevalent. Major news media continue to tell of incorrect credit reports, errors in large computer files, and other horror stories begun by inaccurate computer data, and the World Wide Web is now being used by numerous organizations to gather customer information. The 1995 Columbia Pictures film *The Net* seemed to speak directly to the fears of the MarketPlace protesters when the main character, caught up in a scenario in which personal information about her was being abused by cyberterrorists, described with panic and fear how her entire personal history was available on the Internet. This concern was still in the air when, in 1993, the White House announced the Clipper chip.

3 The Case of the Clipper Chip

Like the protest over Lotus MarketPlace, the online action against the Clipper chip was preceded by activity by privacy experts and activists. The controversy over the Clipper chip, however, is actually based on a long history of governmental interest in a standardized encryption design. The Computer Security Act of 1987 required that the National Institute for Standards and Technology (NIST), a federal standards-setting organization within the Commerce Department, develop a new national standard for computer encryption. This standard would replace the existing data encryption standard, known as DES. Personal electronic devices, including cellular telephones and modems, had increased in power and popularity throughout the 1980s, and communication technologies and networks were predicted to continue this rapid growth. Such growth required an algorithm much more complex than the DES, which was developed in 1977, when few computers existed and when those that were in use were generally not powerful enough to crack the DES algorithm. Unlike the proposed Clipper standard, which requires two keys (each held by a different agency), the DES involved the use of a single key to both encrypt and decrypt a message; by 1987, this design was considered outdated and not sophisticated enough to support the continuing information revolution.

A large part of the government's motive for developing the new standard was to ensure that new technologies did not outpace the ability of federal law enforcement agencies to perform legal surveillance of electronic material, such as tapping phones or intercepting and decoding computer transmissions. If computer and telecommunications companies abandoned the unsophisticated DES, they might instead use any of several new and more complex encryption algorithms, especially if the DES was not replaced by a new governmental standard. Should industries choose these commercial encryption technologies, such agencies as the FBI would be unable to decipher the ever-increasing number of electronic communication transmissions in the United States when they needed to perform such surveillance legally in a criminal investigation.

The NIST followed the directive of the 1987 Computer Security Act and began work on a new federal encryption standard. To do so, it turned to the National Security Agency (NSA), described as "the United States' most secretive intelligence organization." The NSA proceeded to develop an escrowed encryption standard (EES), which would be implemented in a chip that came to be known as Clipper. This chip could be inserted into a telephone handset or fax machine.[1]

On April 16, 1993, President Bill Clinton proposed the EES as the new encryption standard. This announcement triggered immediate concern among privacy advocates, concern that came about as a result of the NSA's secretive behavior and its "long history of resisting industry efforts to develop such technology on the ground that any codes not breakable by the NSA might compromise national security." Furthermore, although the 1987 act stipulated that a public advisory group be consulted during the development of the new standard, the NSA had "largely ignored" this group, working in a highly secretive fashion. In May 1993, CPSR obtained documents through the Freedom of Information Act indicating that the NSA "used the process of technical working groups to wear down opposition by institute scientists who wanted to keep the standard open to scrutiny."

This lack of concern for public input caused such groups as CPSR and the EFF to begin sounding alarms. These groups also worried that the NSA might specify a chip designed with a "trap door" that would allow unauthorized government tapping. Additionally, privacy advocates raised questions about who would hold the keys. As in the Lotus case, media coverage in the *New York Times* and other major newspapers began appearing, highlighting the ideological split between privacy advocates and proponents of the government's proposal.

Industry groups also raised concerns about Clipper—concerns that had little do with privacy but everything to do with the growing global market for high-technology products. "That an obscure technical standard such as the Clipper chip should produce such a backlash reflects how important cryptography has become to the private sector," noted one observer (Carney 1993, 2185). Computer and telecommunications industries, aware of the growing markets for communication technology, argued that no foreign companies would want to purchase products using encryption schemes that could be unscrambled by U.S. investigative agencies. The Clipper standard, they maintained, would be a severe blow to U.S. exports; *Forbes* magazine called it "really a dumb idea," suggesting that "high-tech exports will be devastated" (Forbes 1994, 26). Industry representatives thus joined with privacy advocates to voice continuing opposition to the Clipper chip.

As in the Lotus MarketPlace case, cyberspace was an important forum for discussions, debates, and protests concerning the Clipper chip. Information moved across the Internet via email, Usenet newsgroups, and discussion lists. Special file-transfer protocol (ftp) sites (computer directories set up to allow public access to text and other files) were set up to house important Clipper-related documents, and before long, the Internet was "buzzing with talk of insurrection" about Clipper (Markoff 1994a). The role of the cyberspace forum became so evident that it was noted by an official government publication: in February 1994, shortly after the administration's approval of the Clipper standard, the *Federal Register* published official notice of the standard and, in its analysis of the comments received during the Clipper review period, noted, "Of the 298 comments received from industry organizations and from individuals, 225 were forwarded to NIST from the Electronic Frontier Foundation which had collected them as electronic mail messages" (NIST 1994, 5998). In fact, the information circulated online about Clipper included numerous sample form letters and an electronic petition that could be signed simply by sending an email message.

Some Background on Encryption

A working understanding of encryption technology in general, and the Clipper chip in specific, will help explain the concerns about Clipper.[2] Encryption involves the use of a mathematical algorithm to scramble electronic messages. This algorithm can then be encoded onto a computer chip, which is inserted in the particular device for which the chip was designed. The Clipper chip, for example, can be inserted into a telephone handset. When a phone call was made, the resulting message would be encrypted as it left the caller's telephone. It would then be decrypted when received on the listener's Clipper-equipped telephone. Only the two parties involved in the phone call would be able to understand the original message. Anyone attempting to eavesdrop on the call—a possibility of special concern for cellular phone users—would not be able to understand the conversation unless that individual had access to the keys, or descrambling algorithms, necessary to decipher the message.

The Clinton administration's proposed standard for encryption, the EES, would in theory make messages difficult to crack, as the key would be split in half, with the two halves held in escrow in separate locations (fig. 3.1). Decryption could take place only when both keys were used together. Federal agents wishing to listen in on a phone conversation would have to obtain warrants and present these to each escrow agent in order to obtain both keys. The EES can be employed in a number of devices. Clipper, for example, is an EES chip designed specifically for telephone and fax machines; Capstone (another device proposed by the Clinton administration) would employ the EES standard for computers (Carney 1993). The mathematical algorithm used in the Clipper chip is known as Skipjack.[3]

The Debate over the Clipper Chip

President Clinton's announcement on April 16 was essentially the beginning of a one-year debate about the EES and the Clipper

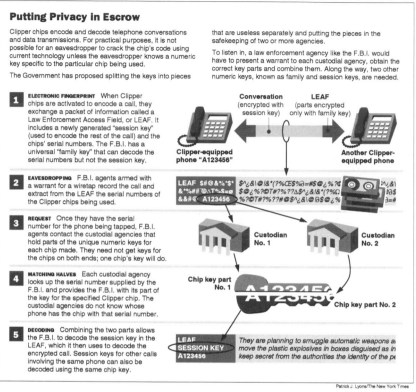

Putting Privacy in Escrow

Clipper chips encode and decode telephone conversations and data transmissions. For practical purposes, it is not possible for an eavesdropper to crack the chip's code using current technology unless the eavesdropper knows a numeric key specific to the particular chip being used.

The Government has proposed splitting the keys into pieces that are useless separately and putting the pieces in the safekeeping of two or more agencies.

To listen in, a law enforcement agency like the F.B.I. would have to present a warrant to each custodial agency, obtain the correct key parts and combine them. Along the way, two other numeric keys, known as family and session keys, are needed.

1 ELECTRONIC FINGERPRINT When Clipper chips are activated to encode a call, they exchange a packet of information called a Law Enforcement Access Field, or LEAF. It includes a newly generated "session key" (used to encode the rest of the call) and the chips' serial numbers. The F.B.I. has a universal "family key" that can decode the serial numbers but not the session key.

Conversation (encrypted with session key)

LEAF (parts encrypted only with family key)

Clipper-equipped phone "A123456"

Another Clipper-equipped phone

2 EAVESDROPPING F.B.I. agents armed with a warrant for a wiretap record the call and extract from the LEAF the serial numbers of the Clipper chips being used.

3 REQUEST Once they have the serial number for the phone being tapped, F.B.I. agents contact the custodial agencies that hold parts of the unique numeric keys for each chip made. They need not get keys for the chips on both ends; one chip's key will do.

Custodian No. 1

Custodian No. 2

4 MATCHING HALVES Each custodial agency looks up the serial number supplied by the F.B.I. and provides the F.B.I. with its part of the key for the specified Clipper chip. The custodial agencies do not know whose phone has the chip with that serial number.

Chip key part No. 1

Chip key part No. 2

5 DECODING Combining the two parts allows the F.B.I. to decode the session key in the LEAF, which it then uses to decode the encrypted call. Session keys for other calls involving the same phone can also be decoded using the same chip key.

LEAF
SESSION KEY
A123456

They are planning to smuggle automatic weapons a, move the plastic explosives in boxes disguised as h keep secret from the authorities the identity of the pe

Patrick J. Lyons/The New York Times

Figure 3.1. The process by which the Clipper chip would function. From Lewis 1994. Copyright © 1994 by the New York Times Company. Reprinted by permission.

chip.[4] Immediately after this announcement, information began appearing in all the major print media and on Internet privacy forums and other electronic lists and newsgroups. The EFF and CPSR posted information, and individuals began to express their concerns. The year-long debate was punctuated by a number of key events, and documentation related to each event was almost immediately available on the Internet, through both ftp sites and the mass circulation of email postings.

On May 6, less than one month after the proposed EES was announced, a group called the Digital Privacy and Security Working Group (DPSWG), which described itself as a "coalition of communication and computer companies and associations and consumer and privacy advocates" coordinated by the EFF, sent a letter to President Clinton. Although the letter applauded the president's "efforts to develop a greater understanding of these complex issues," it also indicated "that there are fundamental privacy and other constitutional rights that must be taken into account when any domestic surveillance scheme is proposed. Moreover, it is unclear how [President Clinton's] proposal and the overall review of cryptography policy will impact on U.S. export controls" (DPSWG 1993). The DPSWG requested a role in the development of encryption policy and raised questions about commercial concerns and privacy in relation to Clipper. The letter was posted on various EFF electronic forums and soon made its way across the Internet. It was prefaced with an introductory paragraph stating "please circulate broadly" in capital letters (which on email indicates shouting) and providing the email address for Jerry Berman of the EFF.

The next month, on June 2, the DPSWG presented a statement as public testimony during two days of hearings held by the Computer System Security and Privacy Advisory Board, a body established by Congress under the 1987 Computer Security Act. This statement used stronger language than the earlier letter, questioning Clipper's economic viability and noting its potentially harmful impact on high-technology business. Marc Rotenberg of CPSR also testified, stating that the "Clipper proposal clearly violates the intent of the Computer Security Act of 1987" by keeping most aspects of the chip closed to public scrutiny (Rotenberg 1993b). Based on these hearings, on June 5 the Computer System Security and Privacy Advisory Board issued two resolutions that posed concerns about the Clipper chip standard and recommended that the standard not be deployed until the complete range of public policy and technical issues were more fully understood. Meanwhile, CPSR had already, on May 28, filed a suit "challenging the secrecy of the government's 'Clipper chip' encryption proposal" by requesting through the Freedom of Information Act the disclosure of all information concerning the EES and Clipper. Because the NSA was developing the algorithm, it was slated to remain secret and not open to public scrutiny, and the CPSR suit was designed to bring the Clipper information to the public.

The DPSWG's statement, Rotenberg's testimony, the final recommendations of the board, and information about CPSR's suit were all posted on the Internet, initially on CPSR forums and relevant mailing lists, then on other Internet sites. These postings highlighted the problems with Clipper and the secrecy and perceived uncooperativeness of the federal government, thus continuing to fuel the online debate and discontent. A CPSR posting entitled "NSA Seeks Delay in Clipper Case," for example, contained the following excerpt from an affidavit by Michael A. Smith, NSA policy director, filed in response to CPSR's suit:

> NSA's search for records responsive to [CPSR's]
> request is under way, but is not yet complete.
> Because the Clipper Chip program is a significant
> one involving the participation of organizations in
> four of NSA's five Directorates and the Director's
> staff, the volume of responsive documents is likely
> to be quite large. Moreover, because the Clipper
> Chip program is highly complex and technical and
> is, in substantial part, classified for national
> security purposes, the review process cannot be
> accomplished quickly. (CPSR 1993)

Discussions continued on the Internet, especially in such electronic spaces as CPSR, EFF, Cypherpunks, and RISKS Digest. On June 7, Raymond Kammer of the NIST announced that the Clipper plan would be delayed until the issues could be studied in more detail (Schwartz 1993), and that the review of the Clipper chip and the EES would be extended into the fall. During this same period, a major conference on cryptography was held, and the issues continued to be debated.

On September 17, administration officials announced the names of the two escrow agents that would hold the respective halves of the key necessary to decipher a message encrypted with Clipper. The agents would be the NIST and a non-law-enforcement agency in the Treasury Department (Mintz and Schwartz 1993). This announcement was broadcast across cyberspace and caused much outcry because these agents were not independent of the federal government.

Debates continued through the fall and early winter. In early December, the DPSWG announced that it would accept Clipper if the standard were voluntary and if tight controls over the exporting of cryptography were dropped. The administration agreed that Clipper would be a voluntary standard, but it was unwilling to compromise on the issue of cryptography export, because the government treated cryptography as a military secret. As a result of these and other factors, a number of companies announced in January 1994 that they would use not Clipper but rather an alternative encryption standard known as RSA (the initials of its three inventors) (Daly 1994; Markoff 1994b). These companies found RSA more appealing because it was a commercially developed algorithm that did not involve the federal government's holding of any escrowed keys. Additionally, on January 24, CPSR coordinated a letter to President Clinton that raised concerns about the secrecy surrounding Clipper's development and ultimately, after citing specific privacy concerns, asked that the White House withdraw the entire Clipper proposal. The letter, signed by forty-one computer privacy advocates, cryptography experts, and technical specialists, was circulated on the Internet with the heading "Crypto Experts Oppose Clipper." Shortly thereafter, CPSR organized an online petition against Clipper, based in part on favorable responses to the letter and multiple requests from people who wished to add their signatures. This petition could be "signed" by simply sending an email message to a CPSR address (Clipper.petition@cpsr.org) with the message "I oppose Clipper." The email address of the sender was then added to the bottom of the letter. The petition garnered between forty and fifty thousand signatures.[5]

Despite the efforts of industry and advocacy groups, the Clinton administration officially adopted the Clipper as a federal information-processing standard for voice communications on February 4, 1994. Although this standard was made voluntary for the private sector, the administration hoped that if it made Clipper the governmental standard, industry would follow suit. One report indicated that the Justice Department had placed an $8 million order for Clipper chips and that the Pentagon was also about to order a large quantity of the encryption devices. Any private companies that wished to do business with the government would ultimately be forced to use the Clipper standard.

Critics continued to question the privacy and economic implications of the government's plan. And although supporters claimed that Clipper would help stop international terrorism, spying, and other criminal behavior, Senator Patrick Leahy and others counterargued that criminals could simply choose not to use Clipper and could instead rely on any of the numerous alternative encryption algorithms that were readily available (Andrews 1994).

Throughout February and March, Clipper continued to make news both in the mass media and on the Internet. On March 11, 1994, the EES and the Clipper chip became effective as a federal encryption standard (NIST 1994).

The Protest in Cyberspace

Along with the main events in the Clipper controversy, most of which quickly reverberated across the Internet, other incidents were taking place on Usenet newsgroups and discussion lists and over private email. Some of these events paralleled the major announcements of the federal government and CPSR or the EFF, and others related directly to the rhetorical dynamics of communities in cyberspace.

Within days of the announcement of the EES and Clipper chip, newsgroups contained a multitude of postings. On April 19, 1993, just three days after the announcement, the online Computer Privacy Digest began with a posting from Dave Banisar of CPSR. This posting, which is actually dated April 16, the same day as Clinton's announcement, is entitled "Computer Professionals Call for Public Debate on New Government Encryption Initiative." In the statement, CPSR raises objections to the development of the encryption standard by the NSA, which it calls a "super-secret military intelligence agency," and announces that it has filed a number of requests under the Freedom of Information Act to obtain more information about the plan.[6] In the same issue of Computer Privacy Digest is a letter written by a private citizen to President Clinton stating this person's concerns with Clipper and suggesting that others also write such letters.[7] Other electronic forums also posted the CPSR announcement and various messages about Clipper from individuals. Such newsgroups as alt.privacy.clipper sprang up in response to the Clipper chip announcement, and such existing groups as the Cypherpunks and talk.politics.crypto began discussing Clipper. Both CPSR and EFF quickly organized ftp sites for public access to important Clipper-related documents.

One online effort to oppose Clipper, the petition organized by CPSR at the end of January 1994, was one of the first of its kind. The petition garnered many signatures, but it also generated discussion about the ethics of using such an approach. Critics claimed that the speed of online delivery allowed anyone to send in a signature quickly without reviewing the facts of the case or truly understanding the complexities of cryptography in general and Clipper and EES in specific (see Chapter 6).

The White House (1993) also used the Internet, responding early on with a lengthy note (posted to a few sites) announcing Clipper and providing answers to what the administration presumed were the major questions about EES and Clipper. In addition, journal articles, conference presentations, and other formal information about Clipper continued to appear on the privacy discussion groups throughout the debate.

Whereas Lotus MarketPlace was primarily a bottom-up effort, the Clipper protest was in large part orchestrated by CPSR and the EFF. Yet the Clipper controversy also included many individual actions. In May 1993, an anonymous Internet user posted what he or she claimed was confidential and detailed information about Mykotronx Corporation, the company hired by the government to produce the Clipper chip.[8] Referring to Mykotronx as the "Big-Brother outfit that is going to make the Clinton Clipper wiretap chip," this posting included specifics about Mykotronx personnel and excerpts from the company's general ledger. The excerpts contained information regarding accounts receivable and accounts payable, and were sprinkled with such comments as "Holy shit—I wish I worked for a place that paid bonuses like that!" Although the posting contained no information about the author's credibility, it was widely circulated, and some saw it as an ironic revenge against a company hired to produce a chip designed to secure electronic data; one reporter noted that a "security problem at Mykotronx is like arson in a firehouse" (Hotz 1993). Similar to the anonymous internal memo from Lotus that was posted to the Internet at the end of the MarketPlace case, the Mykotronx postings illustrate the sense of community felt by those on the Internet, and, at the same time, the problem of ascertaining the accuracy of information in cyberspace.

The many online discussions about Professor Dorothy Denning were another interesting phenomenon. Denning, chair of the computer science department at Georgetown University and an expert on cryptography, was asked by the NSA to evaluate the security features of Clipper. Because Denning generally favored Clipper, her credibility and knowledge were heavily criticized by online privacy communities. Online participants were suspicious of Denning because she worked directly with the mistrusted NSA to perform her evaluation. She often engaged these criticisms in her own Internet postings, and her presence in these debates illustrates the conflicts that result when someone with differing views enters the often self-referential and insular communities on the Internet (see Chapter 7).

Clipper Today

Unlike the Lotus protest, the Clipper online debate had mixed results. On the one hand, the online actions created broad awareness about the proposed encryption standard. On the other hand, despite the CPSR petition, Clipper and the EES were adopted by the government, and the EES remains a voluntary standard in the private sector. The Clipper case thus suggests that claims about the Internet, democracy, and the power of the vox populi must be carefully tempered with considerations of the greater social and political forces at work. The online ethos and electronic delivery so powerful in the Lotus case, in which a private corporation was concerned about profit margins and consumer attitudes, were not as effective in the realm of federal government agencies and presidential decisions.

Clipper and the EES continue to be debated on the Internet and elsewhere. In January 1995, the Association of the Bar of the City of New York held a discussion on Clipper. And in August 1995, the Electronic Privacy Information Center (EPIC), a CPSR-sponsored organization, posted a notice to the Internet describing new findings concerning Clipper and the lack of governmental concern for public input. Corporations continue to protest the export restrictions on encryption, and Clipper and the EES remain controversial topics on the privacy forums of the Internet. Encryption will continue to be an important topic as communication technology advances and expands into almost every sector of society.

4 Exigence in Cyberspace

In both the MarketPlace and Clipper cases, discussions and protests got off to a quick start, within twenty-four hours of the announcement of each respective technology. In this chapter I analyze the forces and events behind the early discussions and formation of online communities specific to MarketPlace and Clipper. These online debates developed because both products were introduced against a social and historical background of concern over computer privacy, and, in this context, the rhetorical dynamics of delivery and ethos in cyberspace aided in bringing the discussions into focus.

By the end of the 1980s, when MarketPlace was announced, issues of computers and personal privacy were much in the public eye. Computer professionals were especially aware of the potential privacy problems associated with computers, and when Market-Place was released, these people turned to the communication methods available in cyberspace to distribute their opinions and ideas. Later, when the Clipper chip was announced, similar concerns about computers, privacy, and government were still in place, enhanced by the outcry over MarketPlace just two years before. Again, these concerns set the stage for rapid and far-reaching discussions and actions in cyberspace.

Communication on the Internet is profoundly different from anything yet experienced in communication technology. Only television has a similarly broad reach, but it is noninteractive and non-selective: everyone receives the same information with no option for feedback. In contrast, the quick, broad, and specialized reach of computer-mediated communication, along with the ability for user interaction, provides for an unprecedented rhetorical forum.

The cases of Lotus MarketPlace and the Clipper chip both offered the opportunity for a rhetorical situation, or what can be thought of as a "complex of persons, events, objects, and relations

presenting an actual or potential exigence which can be . . . removed if discourse, introduced into the situation, can so constrain
human decision or action as to bring about a significant modification of the exigence." The first constituent of any rhetorical situation is, in fact, an exigence: "an imperfection marked by urgency"
(Bitzer 1968, 6).[1] In the cases of MarketPlace and Clipper, the exigence involved a technology that many perceived as imperfect and
dangerous, and this exigence was defined and focused through the
dynamics of communication in cyberspace.

The Lotus and Clipper cases suggest that in cyberspace, exigencies form in two stages and move through these stages quickly.
First, a general concern exists in the public mind. This concern
then comes into focus through what in classical rhetoric is the
kairotic, or opportune, introduction of a representative product,
concept, or other tangible symbol. In the late 1980s, for example,
increasing concerns emerged about personal privacy in relation to
computers. By the end of the 1980s, discussions of computers and
personal privacy were widespread. Lotus MarketPlace acted as a
catalyst, or lightning rod, on which the exigence could then focus as
individuals began using the Internet to talk about MarketPlace. In
other words, MarketPlace gave people the "mobilization exigency"
around which to organize their concerns about computer privacy.
Such exigence has been argued to help distinguish the "rhetorical
situation of movements" and protests from other rhetorical situations (Smith and Windes 1976). As one privacy advocate put it,
the MarketPlace protest community was "like kindling waiting for
a spark" (Rotenberg 1992); MarketPlace, and later Clipper, provided that needed spark.

Yet sparks do not become flames unless they are fanned and
given the proper fuel; that is, exigencies do not form apart from
human action. In the Lotus and Clipper cases, this action was
enhanced and speeded up by the use of the Internet to provide
information about initial investigations and advocacy work of computer privacy organizations, specifically CPSR. In the Lotus case,
CPSR was involved in early advocacy efforts and was partly responsible for the major media coverage, which then spawned the online

protest. In the Clipper case, CPSR played an even greater role, creating and maintaining many online information sources (via ftp and the World Wide Web) and collecting signatures for its online petition (see Chapter 5 for a detailed discussion of the structural differences between the two protests).

In both cases, the exigence came into focus through an interaction of three forces. First, a general background of concern about computer privacy in the United States was already in place at the time of the announcement of MarketPlace and was even stronger and more prevalent when the Clipper chip was introduced. Second, the speed and reach of online delivery helped bring information to interested network users within hours and sometimes even minutes. Finally, online community members in both cases shared an ethos; this ethos involved a hostile, authoritative persona and a prevailing sense of technical assuredness and competency.

Concerns about Computer Privacy in the United States

Ever since the first computer was constructed, people have expressed concern about the potential privacy problems that could be caused by the unregulated use of machines to track and monitor information.[2] In general, the issue of privacy in the United States has always been a complicated one. Although privacy was described by Justice Louis Brandeis as the "most comprehensive of rights," the Bill of Rights does not specifically use the word *privacy*.[3] However, the 1965 Supreme Court decision *Griswold v. Connecticut* established privacy as a constitutional guarantee (Trubow 1991, 19–3). In casual conversation, Americans often invoke their "right to privacy." Yet this right is not clear-cut. Bennett (1992), noting that "it is impossible to list a definitive and exhaustive set of concerns encompassed by the word 'privacy,'" calls privacy a "notoriously vague, ambiguous, and controversial term that embraces a confusing knot of problems, tensions, rights, and duties" (13). These problems, he says, span a range of issues from abortion to governmental or police surveillance to data collection (13). Computers, with their power and speed, have amplified concerns about this last issue by providing a historically unprecedented ability to collect, maintain, and use data about private citizens.

Early in the development of computers, such scientists as Joseph Weizenbaum (1976) raised concerns about the potential dangers of computer use. These concerns echoed Jacques Ellul's (1964) earlier, more general fear of the abuse of *la technique* (*"methods rationally arrived at and having absolute efficiency* . . . in *every* field of human activity"* [xxv]) but were specifically focused on computer technology. In his classic *Computer Power and Human Reason* (1976), Weizenbaum describes the dangers of using the computer as an analogy for human thought. Such a rational analogy, he argues, could easily lead us toward a disregard for ethical issues. Computers, he says, have "merely reinforced and amplified those antecedent pressures that have driven man to an ever more highly rationalistic view of his society and an ever more mechanistic image of himself" (238).

The 1970s and 1980s saw an increase in concern about computer privacy, in part because of the increased use of computers by governmental and private organizations. Alan Westin's (1972) work in the early 1970s sought to provide an overview and raise awareness of the role of computers and other "information technologies" in relation to privacy. Other work, such as David Burnham's (1980) *Rise of the Computer State*, Kenneth Laudon's (1986) *Dossier Society*, and James Rule's (1974) *Private Lives and Public Surveillance*, continued to highlight social and organizational issues about computer privacy. Some scholars (such as Deborah Johnson [1985]) began to call for consideration of computer ethics as a way to address the growing concerns about computers and personal privacy.

Newspaper and magazine articles during the 1980s brought the issue of computer privacy to the public's attention. Cartoons anthropomorphized the computer and made it, as the holder of all knowledge, the agent to blame for mistakes on, for example, a person's banking statement. By the late 1980s, the general perception that personal privacy was being invaded by computers was highlighted by such magazine articles as " 'Big Brother Inc.' May Be Closer Than You Thought," which described the "latest threat:

personal 'profiles' compiled from the widening web of databases" (Field et al. 1987, 84), and cover stories like "Is Nothing Private?: Computers Know More About You Than You Realize—and Now Anyone Can Tap In" (Rothfeder 1989). Finally, lawsuits over inaccurate information brought by individuals against the credit-reporting giant TRW in the late 1980s provided the public with an example of what can happen when computerized data is misused. In regard to these trends, data privacy expert David Flaherty (1989) noted that "casual perusal of any newspaper indicates the extent to which problems of personal privacy of the most pressing sort remain in the public eye. People sense that they have lost control over the protection of their own privacy in a world dominated by computers, even if most individuals are as yet only vaguely aware of the real social cost and implications of dossiers on each of us" (6).

Lotus MarketPlace was introduced into this climate of public concern about computer privacy.[4] Computer experts themselves held more specialized views of both the potential benefits and the potential dangers of computers in regard to personal privacy. In the early 1980s CPSR was formed, in response to the potential social dangers of computer use, by computer scientists who wished to "integrate their work life into their social concerns."[5] Like Weizenbaum and others in the early days of computing, CPSR members sought to integrate concern about social issues, including privacy, into the development and use of computer technology. By the time of the Lotus announcement in 1990, computer conferences devoted entirely to issues of computers and privacy—such as alt.privacy and comp.society.privacy—existed on the Internet and other networks.

It seems no coincidence, then, that some of the early electronic messages about Lotus MarketPlace were posted to conferences that focus on computers and privacy: RISKS Digest, a conference sponsored by the Committee on Computers and Public Policy of the Association for Computing Machinery (ACM); and a subtopic of the Electronic Frontier Foundation conference on the WELL network. Participants in these conferences had a special interest in computers and computer privacy, and they also had access to and expertise in using the Internet. Furthermore, one Lotus official claimed that the people debating MarketPlace on the networks were "big users of Lotus software" (former Lotus employee B 1993) and therefore had insight into the mechanics of the MarketPlace product.

Concerns about computer privacy only increased after Market-Place, and by the time the Clipper chip was announced in 1993, the online privacy community was even more established. Furthermore, personal computers and the Internet were being used by many more people than in the early 1980s, and the news media and popular press were even more active in their reporting on the potential dangers of computer communication technology in relation to personal privacy. When Clipper was announced, media coverage almost paralleled the language that had been used to describe Lotus MarketPlace. Columnist William Safire (1994), for example, noted that the " 'clipper chip' . . . would encode, for Federal perusal whenever a judge rubber-stamped a warrant, everything we say on a phone, everything we write on a computer, every order we give to a shopping network. . . . Combine [this personal data] with the travel, shopping and credit card data available from all our plastic cards, along with psychological and student test scores. Throw in confidential tax returns, sealed divorce proceedings, welfare records, field investigations for job applications, raw files and C.I.A. dossiers . . . and you have the individual citizen standing naked to the nosy bureaucrat" (17). This commentary is a mixture of concerns about Clipper and encryption, marketing information (similar to what MarketPlace contained), and other general, slightly hyperbolic fears ("sealed divorce proceedings") about computers and privacy. But the sentiment exhibited in Safire's column reflected feelings that many Americans shared at the time of the Lotus and later Clipper announcements. Online delivery and ethos, functioning within this context, helped bring a sharp and immediate focus to the issues.

Online Delivery and Exigence

The *Wall Street Journal* article of November 13, 1990, which resulted in part from the efforts of CPSR earlier that year, inspired many of the early postings in the Lotus protest. In many computer conferences, excerpts from this article appeared almost immediately. The November 16 issue of RISKS Digest, an online newsletter focusing on risks to the public in computing, for example, contained three postings about Lotus MarketPlace, thus illustrating how quickly information can be disseminated into the specialized community spaces on the Internet. The first posting began as follows:

```
Date: Wed, 14 Nov 90 09:19:28 EDT
From: [George M——] [email address deleted]
Subject: Police technology; mailing list hyperstacks

The Wall Street Journal this week had two articles
on privacy and technology that I thought RISKS
readers might find of interest.⁶
```

This posting, included in the November 16 issue of RISKS, is dated November 14, indicating it was actually sent to the Digest just one day after the *Wall Street Journal* article appeared. On the EFF forum on the WELL network, the first posting concerning the Lotus controversy is also dated November 14 and is a reference to the *Journal* article:

```
Topic 71—New Lotus product puts millions of
Americans under scrutiny.
by [Tom K——] [email address deleted] Wed, Nov 14,
1990 (01:33) 292 responses

Tuesday's (10/13) WALL STREET JOURNAL carried a
Section B front page story about Lotus Corporation's
new product. The name escapes me, but the product is
a disk(s) with the names of millions of Americans,
categorized by demographics and buying habits.⁷
```

[The date of 10/13 is obviously a typographical
error and should be 11/13.]

By simply typing a message and issuing the appropriate com-
mands to post it, participants were able to bring the article to the
attention of thousands of readers, if not more, just one day after
the article appeared in the paper. Although the *Journal* has a larger
number of readers than the network conferences, delivery in cyberspace brought the issue of Lotus MarketPlace to the attention of a
specific audience: people with a concern for computer privacy who
knew how to use the networks to spread a message.

It is impossible to say how many people saw these and other
early postings. A reasonable count can be made of the average number of readers to certain computer conferences, but it is impossible
to know how many people saw the postings by way of secondary
sources. Anyone who read the RISKS article, for example, could
copy the message from the conference and redistribute it via email
or repost it to an internal company bulletin board. What is important about delivery in cyberspace thus is much more than the
speed of electronic postings; it is also the exponential process of
cutting and pasting messages from one site to another and passing
these messages along to numerous other cyberspaces.[8]

The second posting to the November 16 issue of RISKS Digest
also exhibits this rapid and far-reaching delivery. In this example,
information about MarketPlace originated on an internal company
network of a large New England computer manufacturer and was
then posted to RISKS Digest via the Internet:

Date: Wed, 14 Nov 90 09:53:47 PST
From: [Geoff P——] [email address deleted]
Subject: Privacy concerns about new Lotus
''Marketplace'' product

The following is extracted from an unofficial
electronic newspaper edited and published within
[large computer company] for [large computer
company] employees. Reproduced with permission. The

issues raised herein should be familiar to regular
RISKS readers.[9]

What followed was an article about Lotus MarketPlace, titled "New Program Spurs Fears Privacy Could Be Undermined," from the internal electronic newsletter of the author's employer. The publication date of the newsletter was November 14, 1990. No sooner did the newsletter make it out to the company's employees than someone reposted this internal story to RISKS Digest, where it could be read by people throughout the Internet.

The third posting to RISKS Digest provides another example of how material in the Lotus case was forwarded and reposted in cyberspace:

```
Date: Thu, 15 Nov 90 09:47:13 -0800
From: [Stan Jacob A——] [email address deleted]
Subject: all US consumers on CD-ROM

This was forwarded to me: [Discussion of PBS item on
Lotus deleted. PGN]

    The database does not contain any of the data
covered by the fair credit practices act so Lotus is
under no legal obligation to let you see what they
are saying about you (unless you buy the product, of
course . . . ) and has no provision for allowing you
to change what is in there.
    The Lotus spokesman said that if people wrote a
letter to Lotus saying they did not want to be in the
database, they would be excluded. Unfortunately, the
interviewer did not say to whom the letter should be
addressed.[10]
```

The author of this note took material that had been forwarded to him and reposted this material to RISKS Digest along with his own commentary. The first line, "this was forwarded to me," indicates that in the original posting, the author had attached a message that had been forwarded to him from another source. The bracketed "Discussion of PBS item on Lotus deleted. PGN" is an insertion from the moderator of RISKS Digest (Peter G. Neuman) indicating that he edited out the forwarded material.[11] The final two paragraphs are the commentary of the author.

Thus, within twenty-four hours after the *Wall Street Journal* article appeared, word had spread throughout cyberspace about the Lotus product, and before long, discussion groups focusing on MarketPlace had sprung up across the Internet. Because it is so easy to forward and repost notes to computer conferences or as email, delivery in cyberspace helped the controversy come into sharp focus quickly.

In the Clipper case, a similar form of delivery took place, quickly bringing together like-minded individuals into a community against the adoption of the chip. Shortly after the Clinton administration proposed the Clipper chip as a voluntary standard for telecommunications encryption in April 1993, a number of advocacy groups began to organize. The Digital Privacy and Security Working group, for example, composed of a "coalition of communication and computer companies and associations, and consumer and privacy advocates," was formed in May; this group sent a letter to President Clinton questioning the Clipper chip. Also in May, CPSR sent a letter to President Clinton, stating that the group disagreed with some statements of the Digital Privacy and Security Working group. Later in May, CPSR filed a suit "challenging the secrecy of the government's Clipper chip encryption proposal" (CPSR 1993).

All these activities were discussed and monitored on the Internet. As in the Lotus case, specialized Usenet newsgroups, such as alt.privacy.clipper, formed quickly. Other newsgroups focusing on computers and privacy soon contained discussions, or "threads," about the Clipper chip. On April 16, the day of the administration's announcement of the proposed standard, the statement by the White House press secretary was available on many Internet sites. The statement was widely reposted, appearing, for example, in the April 27 issue of the online Computer Privacy Digest. Also on April 16, CPSR posted an announcement calling for a public debate on the issue; this message was widely cross-posted, appearing in the April 16 issue of the Privacy Forum Digest, the April 19 issue of Computer Privacy Digest, and the April 21 issue of RISKS Digest.

The following message offers an example of the process and power of reposting in electronic delivery, similar to the reposting in the early stages of the Lotus case. The header information of this message, dated Saturday, April 17, provides a trail of the message as it traveled to the newsgroup alt.internet.services and was subsequently copied to the Computer Privacy Digest:

```
Date: Sat, 17 Apr 93 14:04:30 -0700
From: [Earl S——] [email address deleted]
Subject: Clipper Chip

Hello, I recently read this in alt.internet.services
and thought it would be appropriate to cross-post.

From: [email address deleted] [name deleted]
Newsgroups: alt.internet.services
Subject: Computer Security
Message-ID: <1993Apr17.021904.27040@csus.edu>
Date: 17 Apr 93 02:19:04 GMT
Sender: news@csus.edu
Organization: San Francisco State University
Lines: 311

Just thought some of you netters might be interested
in this one. Please direct follow-ups to sci.crypt.[12]
```

What followed was a copy of the White House press release of April 16 announcing the Clipper initiative.

Another participant also mentions this cross-posting, again illustrating how delivery in cyberspace helped to focus the initial exigence. Noting that he has obtained a faxed copy of a Clipper-related letter from Representative Edward Markey to Secretary of Commerce Ron Brown, the author of this posting indicates he has attached a copy of this letter to his posting and describes where he plans to send the letter across the Internet:

```
I'm sending this to a few people (via BCC [blind
carbon copy]) and to a few mailing lists (listed in
the TO line) related to privacy, encryption, clipper
chip, etc. I'll also be posting this to the
sci.crypt and alt.clipper newsgroups. Because of the
traffic on some of the mailing lists, if you have a
comment for me you should email directly to me.13
```

By May, postings about the Clipper chip were quickly making their way across the Internet into such places as the Computer Privacy Digest, the Cypherpunks list, and other computer privacy-related newsgroups and discussion lists. Much as in the Lotus case, these notes were bounced far and wide across the Internet, as noticed by the following participant:

```
Date: Tue, 20 Apr 93 10:45 GMT [RISKS-14.51]
From: [R. N——] [email address deleted]
Subject: Clinton's Clipper Chip Chaos

As soon as the official press release on the Clipper
chip was posted a barrage of posts concerned with
the safety and RISKS of said chip smothered
the net.14
```

This "barrage of posts" involved many newsgroups—such as alt.privacy.clipper, comp.org.eff.talk, sci.crypt, and alt.security— within a short time. Within a few days, an online computer privacy community specifically interested in Clipper had begun to develop. Newsgroups and lists were founded for the sole purpose of discussing the Clipper chip; the newsgroup alt.privacy.clipper, for example, was (and is) devoted entirely to conversations about Clipper. The Cypherpunks forum had regular threads of Clipper-based discussion, and both CPSR and EFF had online spaces devoted to Clipper.

In both the MarketPlace and Clipper cases, speed and simultaneous delivery assisted in focusing the online communities quickly. These communities of common interest would have taken months or even longer to organize through traditional rhetorical means or even through more modern forms such as direct mail. But delivery in cyberspace assisted in bringing people together within hours or days of important events and provided accessible meeting places that spanned distance and time for communities of mutual interest.

Community Ethos and Exigence

Speed of delivery alone will not move people to action. In cyberspace, it was the combination of electronic delivery and a strong community ethos that focused both protests in their early stages. This ethos was a combination of shared technical values and shared attitudes toward the technology in question. Lotus MarketPlace discussants expressed a hostile, angry ethos because the product presented what they felt was a personal threat. Clipper chip discussants also shared an angry attitude toward the technology, but they focused more heavily on the nature of the technology. In both cases, the rhetorical dynamic of a shared community ethos was important in focusing the early postings into cohesive online protests.

The highly specialized virtual spaces on the Internet make it easy to join a community and quickly understand and assume the community ethos; a newsgroup focused on computer privacy, for example, is most likely to be inhabited by participants who are concerned about privacy and want to protect their rights. Often, participants do not have to spend time making introductory remarks or defending the premises of their statements. This "instant ethos" makes it easy to reach many individuals of similar values in short order, and when combined with online delivery allowed for both protests to focus quickly. Participants in the protests were able to assume that others in the newsgroups or lists understood certain technical concepts and agreed with certain premises. The first posting in the MarketPlace case to RISKS Digest is a good example of the beginnings of a community ethos, one that reflects an understanding of technology and an attitude about computers and privacy. This posting, dated November 14, 1990, and beginning with the statement "The Wall Street Journal this week had two articles on privacy and technology that I thought RISKS readers might find of interest," continues:

On Tuesday (14-Nov; page B1) the Journal reports on the controversy surrounding a product soon to be introduced by Lotus. Lotus Marketplace consists of a CD containing information on some 80,000,000 households, including names, addresses, shopping habits, likely income levels, and even a categorization (by Equifax) into one of 50 categories like ''accumulated wealth,'' ''mobile home families,'' ''cautious young couples,'' and ''inner-city singles.'' Also included is a program—apparently at least partly a Hypercard stack—that provides an interface to the system. The whole thing costs $695 for the program and an initial 5000 names; each additional 5000 names cost $400. How Lotus keeps you from using the other information on the CD is unclear—presumably, you sign a license and they come after you if you breach the terms.

The program Lotus provides does not allow you to look up a particular individual by name, but of course if you know anything about him you can come up with a query that will find him and few others—and of course the unethical will hardly be stopped from developing their own search programs by the terms of a license agreement.

All of this information has been available for some time from mailing-list vendors. However, it's been expensive and ''transient.'' What Lotus does is provide the information permanently and cheaply. Lotus says that to prevent abuse, they will not include telephone numbers (of course, CD's with telephone number listings are increasingly available) and will sell only to ''legitimate businesses'' at verified addresses checked against a

```
''fraud file.'' The license terms will limit the
uses to which the data can be put and provide
penalties for abuses. It astonishes me that anyone
can imagine they can control how a small piece of
plastic, indistinguishable from hundreds of like
copies, will be used once it gets out into
the world.¹⁵
```

These phrases reflect this participant's assumptions about other community members. First, the author reveals his expertise as a computer professional and makes assumptions about his readers' technical knowledge. In the second paragraph, for example, the phrase "come up with a query" is a technical way to refer to a database strategy for accessing records. The comment "apparently at least partly a Hypercard stack" is another technical phrase. The message writer spends no time explaining these terms, because he assumes his audience will understand.

Second, the use of the phrase "of course" in the second paragraph acknowledges that the audience will naturally accept and agree with the premise of these comments: that unethical people do exist and do represent a threat to privacy with regard to the Lotus product. Lotus officials would probably not have agreed with this premise and would not have accepted the "of course" in this sentence. But the forum of the RISKS Digest assumes that a certain set of values are shared by speaker and audience, values that are reflected in the ethos of this participant.

Finally, in these paragraphs, the author expresses his expertise and opinions about computers and privacy, challenging Lotus's claims in the *Journal* article. The entire message reflects the author's opinion and not the information presented in the *Journal* article. This opinion illustrates an ethos that combines mild sarcasm with authority, as shown by such phrases as "presumably," "of course," and "it astonishes me." The style is a blend between the formal style of a written memo and the conversational style of an oral exchange. In these early postings, the conversational style allowed participants to make their point quickly without devoting a lot of time to formal styles or background material. Also, the authoritative tone reflects an ethos of direct challenge to Lotus and invites other readers to join the conversation at this same level.

This ethos reflects the feel and habits shared by many online communities.[16] In general, these cyberspaces act as locations where people of common interests can come together to share and debate ideas on specific topics. Because the RISKS Digest, for example, is the ACM's electronic forum on "risks to the public in computers and related systems," most readers of RISKS Digest are concerned with computer privacy. Therefore, speakers assume that their audience agrees with certain tacit premises about computer privacy problems. Furthermore, speakers are more comfortable making ironic and sharp-toned comments: as Aristotle said, it is easier to praise Athenians in Athens; in this case, it is easier to argue against Lotus MarketPlace in a computer privacy forum.[17]

The first posting on another MarketPlace-related discussion group shows similar rhetorical patterns. This posting is also dated November 14 and begins with a reference to the *Wall Street Journal* article. It then continues:

```
Lotus claims the new product will simply make it
easier for smaller businesses to engage in the same
direct marketing (e.g., direct mail and tele-
marketing) practices used by larger firms. But is
this in the public interest, to have all of this
personal information float-ing around without
opportunity even for rebuttal and susceptible to
amateur modification? Does evening the playing field
for business create more equity for the persons
whose data is the commodity at issue?
    Lotus says you can get off their disks in the
conventional way, by calling the various direct
marketeers, or by calling Lotus. First you have to
know about it, however, and the removal process is,
so far, unverified.
    It's ironic that the company founded by Mitch
```

Kapor, who has done so much for personal privacy and
commonsense law regarding the rights of information
workers, consumers, and producers, now is foisting
this sweet little package on the American people.
Comments?[18]

This passage begins with tacit assumptions about technical
knowledge and privacy. Just as the previous posting—"of course
the unethical will hardly be stopped"—assumes that someone will
most certainly abuse the Lotus product, the discussion of a possible misuse by "amateur modification" in this posting assumes
that others in the online community not only understand the technical aspects of such a phrase (the ability of someone to crack the
data encryption scheme used by Lotus) but also understand and to
some extent agree with its implications. In other words, this statement assumes a shared belief in "unethical people" who will try
to crack the encryption scheme built into MarketPlace. Lotus Corporation representatives might have argued with the basis of the
implicit argument of such phrases, suggesting that the encryption
scheme cannot be broken and that no one would want to do such
a thing because this information is already available from other
sources; the participants in these online privacy communities, however, assume this unstated information as a given.

These premises about privacy are also apparent in the questions
that end the first paragraph of the previous quotation. The suggestion that having "all of this personal information floating around"
is a problem, for example, again reflects the values that this writer
assumes are common in the privacy community. By way of contrast, a community of direct-mail marketing professionals would
probably not make this sort of statement. Note the following excerpts from an editorial that appeared in the trade magazine *Direct
Marketing* in May 1990:

It's in this environment that we marvel at the onrush of new
technology . . . databases on CD-ROM, mass faxes. If you
read our . . . weekly newsletter you already know about the
remarkable developments of Donnelly Marketing with their

household file of 80 million names on CD-ROM . . . You
already know what Lotus is up to.
    Lotus announced on April 9 that they would make avail-
able by mid-year both consumer and business databases on
CD-ROM. And you'll be able to buy the . . . databases on
disks . . . for just $695 for either, $1,390 for both, at your
local computer store! Astounding!! . . .
    I am very excited about the future of direct marketing.
(Hoke 1990)

Those who "marvel at the onrush of new technology" have very different premises than those who are concerned about having "all of
this personal information floating around." The two phrases reflect
the ethos of two different points of view: direct mail marketers and
other businesspeople were excited about the possibility of using a
product like MarketPlace, whereas participants in the online privacy community saw MarketPlace as a potential danger.

    The November 14 posting illustrates the sarcastic voice that
was a defining characteristic of the MarketPlace protest community ethos. Note, for example, the phrase "It's ironic that the company . . . now is foisting this sweet little package on the American
people". Furthermore, this posting shows the speaker's authority
in challenging Lotus, as well as his technical expertise, when he
asks, "Is this in the public interest, to have all of this personal information float-ing around without opportunity even for rebuttal
and susceptible to amateur modification?" The phrase "amateur
modification" attacks Lotus's claims that the product had ade-
quate privacy protection. It also illustrates the participant's awareness of nonprofessional people with computer skills, people often
called "hackers" or, more accurately, "crackers" for their interest
in cracking code regardless of the outcome of such activity.

    Assumptions about technical knowledge and computer privacy
in the Lotus case thus allowed for the creation of short, direct messages that assumed the community ethos and would appeal to the
readers of these computer conferences. In addition, an authoritative and ironic voice offered a strong challenge to Lotus's claims

and invited other readers to join the debate. Participants in the two postings analyzed above spoke to a community with whom they shared technical expertise and values about computer privacy. This community ethos, combined with the speed of electronic delivery, played a major role in the initial exigence that developed around the Lotus product.

The early postings in the Clipper case also exhibit the beginning of a strong community ethos, which differed from the ethos of the Lotus protest community in its more technical approach but shared with the Lotus community a rhetorical configuration: "a characteristic manner of holding and expressing ideas" (Halloran 1984, 71), which was powerful because of the highly specialized nature of online spaces and the reach and speed of electronic delivery. The early messages concerning Clipper used highly technical language; for example, in response to the April 16 announcement of Clipper, one participant posted a series of questions to others in the privacy community. These questions clearly assume a certain level of technical knowledge ("V.32 modem;" "Huffman compression") even though the author admits in the beginning of his message that he "isn't a cryptographer and doesn't play one on TV":

> 1. What's an ''encryption'' device? Is a V.32 modem
> one? Without another modem it's pretty hard to
> figure out what's going on. What about programs such
> as compress? With out the ''key'' of the compress/
> decompress program it's a bit difficult to decode
> compressed files. . . .
>   5. What if I use some sort of Huffman compression
> and transmit the frequency table in a separate
> message? Common algorithm but without the ''key'' in
> the form of a frequency table it'll be a bit
> difficult to figure out.[19]

Another early Clipper-related message, posted on Sunday, April 18, invokes the same technical ethos and community awareness of other readers when the author indicates,

As you may know, for some years I have been pushing
for a token-pin-challenge based encryption system
for session as well as password encryption & this
IMHO answers many questions posed by the CC.[20]

Similarly, by suggesting that others reread rather than simply read a certain text, the following author assumes that his audience is familiar with certain texts and has a technical understanding of such issues as the ACM Turing Award:

I think that now would be a good time for all to reread Ken Thompson's ''Reflections on Trusting
Trust,'' which was published as an ACM Turing Award
lecture and appears in a collection book called
''ACM Turing Award lectures: the first twenty years,
1966 to 1985,'' ACM Press, New York, 1987.[21]

The assumptions reflected in this community ethos are probably accurate, because newsgroups and other online forums attract people with such specialized professional backgrounds, interests, and political points of view. Along with technical language, the community ethos in the Clipper protest involved a level of sarcasm and anger similar to the Lotus protest. The first section of a posting from the April 27 issue of the Computer Privacy Digest, for example, reveals its author's overt feelings about Clipper:

DEFEAT THE BIG BROTHER PROPOSAL! JUST SAY F!CK NO TO
THE PRIVACY CLIPPER![22]

This message exhibits the community ethos in its anger and concern over Big Brother and relates this concern to Clipper, which it sarcastically calls the "privacy Clipper." Other early postings in the Clipper case contained similar language:

The idea of registered key systems, where government
and/or LE agencies have involvement, is not a
popular one. The key escrow scheme in this proposal
reeks of Big Brother. (As in, ''Trust me. I'm from

```
the government and I'm your friend.'') In some
circles, it is not even a consideration.²³
```

Another participant, after noting that the key escrow feature of Clipper could pose a threat to personal privacy, sent an email letter to President Clinton, which he subsequently posted to the Computer Privacy Digest. This letter contains a representative statement of the overall community concern about government intervention into personal privacy:

```
This would be an unacceptable erosion of our current
rights, especially of the fundamental right of
privacy which you supported so strongly during your
campaign. Legislation to this effect would be
unenforceable. It would be easily and frequently
broken—leading to the danger that some law
enforcement officer with a private grudge would have
an easy method of filing a criminal complaint
against the innocent victim of his grudge.²⁴
```

Exigence and Community in Cyberspace

Every day, policies and products are announced that are, by someone's standards, deserving of protest. Yet the move from an undefined general problem to focused debate is critical if an issue is to take on broad appeal and become what has been called a rhetorical situation (Bitzer 1968). When Lotus MarketPlace was announced in the spring of 1990, there already existed a background of concern about privacy protection for computerized personal data. MarketPlace gave this general concern a tangible focal point and thus gave shape to a rhetorical exigence. Online protesters in both the MarketPlace and Clipper chip cases used the speed and reach of delivery in cyberspace to put an even sharper focus on the issues.

Privacy advocates viewed the technologies of MarketPlace and Clipper as representing a vision of "computer as Big Brother," and they responded quickly and with strong feeling to this vision. Their actions demonstrate that the power of online communication can be used to control, which concerned the participants in the debates, but at the same time the online discussions show that this communication can also be used to focus and shape an alternative vision. Nevertheless, the highly technical language and specialized nature of the discussion lists and newsgroups encourages a particular kind of community, one that may exclude or inhibit the participation of those who do not share the community knowledge or vision.

As the online debates progressed, they began to exhibit structures of communication which suggest that communication and community in cyberspace are complex and are influenced by a merging of external forces with the intrinsic characteristics of computer-mediated communication. Online petitions, email correspondence with such individuals as the CEO of Lotus or the president of the United States, and anonymous communications in cyberspace are the central components of this structure, and the next chapter analyzes these unique and dynamic elements of communication in cyberspace.

5 Structures of Online Communication

As the MarketPlace and Clipper debates progressed beyond their initial stages, certain texts became widely distributed. In the protest over MarketPlace, the most prominent posting was the Seiler letter, which, although initially posted to only a few sites, was soon widely available on the Internet as participants copied and reposted it. In the Clipper case, CPSR's electronic petition and letter to stop Clipper were also widely distributed. In both cases, these texts became representative of the debate at large and created cohesion among participants across the Internet. The two cases, however, were different in subtle but important ways. MarketPlace was very much a bottom-up action, driven by a few individual postings that held such strong appeal that they were reposted widely and thus provided a cohesion based on community consensus. The Clipper debate was a blend of both top-down and bottom-up structures, organized and maintained by the postings of CPSR and EFF but also sustained via subsequent repostings and additional postings from many individuals.

Once participants learned of MarketPlace and later Clipper, they could and did easily use email to write directly to powerful individuals, bypassing traditional hierarchical structures. In addition, some participants took advantage of the ability to write anonymous postings, broadcasting such information as a purported internal press release from Lotus and, in the Clipper case, supposedly confidential information from the manufacturer of the chips. These anonymous postings, like the messages to higher-ups, circumvented traditional gatekeeping structures and allowed information to move out into a broad forum. Yet the characteristics of these two kinds of electronic communication reveal differences between the two protests and, in the case of the anonymous postings, introduce the problem of inaccurate information (see Chapter 6).

As the debates continued, they exhibited similarities in their uses of delivery and ethos for a successful and wide-reaching online action. Participants in both protests used email to flatten hierarchies and speak to thousands of others across distance and time. Yet the differences in how texts became dominant in the Market-Place and Clipper cases illustrate the range of rhetorical possibilities for online communities and make clear the simplicity and inaccuracy of overly generalized statements about cyberspace as either a new forum for the vox populi and individual expression or as the death knell for community and freedom. Such statements tend toward technological determinism by suggesting that Internet technology alone can create or reduce the opportunity for free expression, when in fact, as these cases show, online communication is shaped not only by hardware and software but also by the external organizational and social forces that are always at work in the greater culture. Lobbying groups like CPSR and EFF, for example, used many traditional tactics (press releases, petitions, and so on) to distribute their message in top-down fashion, while in the MarketPlace debate, notes were posted by many individual participants acting on their own. Each case can justifiably be called a community action in cyberspace, but each offers a different model for how such action might take place. The technology alone is not the determinant of communication-related behavior online.

The technical content and broader social context of the issue being debated also dictate what form of action takes places online. The MarketPlace and Clipper protests suggest that information in cyberspace, in order to engage others, must have a strong initial appeal and be easy to understand and process at a glance. Market-Place was perceived to be a threat to individuals, and the issue was understandable without much research ("my name and spending habits on a CD-ROM"); the protest began within days of Lotus's announcement. In contrast, encryption and the Clipper chip were much more technically complex issues and presented a rather abstract threat to individuals, which explains why the action against the chip did not take on full strength for eight months after its announcement, despite some individual efforts to the contrary. Online participants did not initially react strongly to the complex, lengthy announcements about Clipper, and it took the organizational efforts of CPSR and EFF to structure the debate in a way that was understandable and easy to access. Participants could quickly read and sign CPSR's anti-Clipper petition, which was much simpler than analyzing all the technical material.

When the MarketPlace and Clipper protests moved from their initial stages into full-scale debates, the forces at work in shaping communication structures in cyberspace became clear.[1] These structures reveal how the notion of privacy among advocates on the Internet is closely related to their sense of community. Although participants in the MarketPlace protest, for example, were adamant about having their names removed from the database, some of these participants did not mind having their names and affiliations (and, in the case of one person, an actual home address) traversing freely throughout cyberspace. For these participants, it was a matter of choice: Lotus did not ask for permission to use their names, yet they *chose* to send their postings across the network. It was also a matter of trust in what people thought of as the Internet community, a concept that is revealed in the form of anonymous postings.

How Online Texts Became Dominant

Almost immediately after the initial postings about Lotus MarketPlace, a number of individuals simultaneously posted notes suggesting how Lotus could be contacted. On November 14, one day after the *Wall Street Journal* article appeared, the first posting to one electronic conference included the following paragraph:

```
Lotus says you can get off their disks in the
conventional way, by calling the various direct
marketeers, or by calling Lotus. First you have to
```

```
know about it, however, and the removal process is,
so far, unverified.²
```

Similar postings occurred on other electronic forums as well. These postings were quickly followed by ones that actually provided Lotus's address; the following message, for example, was posted on November 16:

```
Lotus claims that if you don't want to be in the
database you can write a letter to:
Lotus Development Corp.
Attn: Market Name Referral Service
55 Cambridge Parkway
Cambridge, MA 02142³
```

Five days later, another posting contained Lotus's address:

```
You can send your name to Lotus, 55 Cambridge
Parkway, Cambridge, MA 02142 ATTN: Lotus Marketplace
to have your name removed from future editions. Or
so I believe. I will do so tomorrow.⁴
```

Before long, postings shifted from simple address listings to more motivated desires for group action. One participant asked, for example, "Maybe we should generate a mass letter? If so, I'm in."[5] When someone else replied, "If indeed they will remove my name and address, I'm in too,"[6] the original participant made another suggestion of group action protesting MarketPlace:

```
Actually, the idea of taking out a full-page ad
demanding to be removed with a whole lot of
signatures on it and a mail-in coupon to send to
Lotus to demand likewise has a certain charm.
    Time to do a bake sale . . . :-)⁷
```

Further along in the discussion, another participant also expressed interest in a group action, asking if he should write a letter to Lotus or "just support someone else who will write one for all of us."[8] His question was followed up by this posting from Marc Rotenberg of CPSR:

```
If it doesn't bother you, let it pass. If it does,
call Lotus (800/343-5414) and tell them (1) you
would like your name removed, and (2) you think it's
a bad product that shouldn't have been developed.[9]
```

Neither CPSR nor Rotenberg, however, actually produced and circulated such a group letter, as they would later do with the Clipper petition. Instead, the community consensus toward group action was initiated by a number of individuals, whose electronic form letters quickly began to circulate. The most prominent of these was the Seiler letter.

Seiler's note about MarketPlace, which he had downloaded from the Usenet newsgroup news.announce.important and sent to people in his New England computer firm and at other organizations, quickly spread over cyberspace. Seiler says he did not post the note to any conferences or newsgroups, but he did encourage readers to "pass this message along to anyone whom you think might care."[10] The letter traveled extensively.[11] One version was taken from a newsgroup or other Internet source, made its way to British Columbia, was forwarded back to the United States, and was then posted to a new online forum. Embedded in the full posting are header messages indicating that the note had come from an online forum called the Progressive Economists' Network. In that forum, the note was prefaced by the phrase "hold onto your shorts folks, george orwell was only 6 years off," a comment from an online participant whose name is listed only as "kenbo":

```
71, 153 of 292: [Tom K——] [email address deleted]
Thu, Dec 20, 1990 (19:22) 6

The next entry is a long one sent to me by my good
friend S—— S——, who is the policy advocate for the
activist Telecommunications Workers Union, in
British Columbia. He took it off a net somewhere. If
you want to skip it, okay, but I think it's a very
```

juicy rejoinder to Marketplace and the suggested
letter it offers is right on point.

71, 154 of 292: [Tom K——] [email address deleted]
Thu, Dec 20, 1990 (19:27) 212
From apple!cc.sfu.ca!D. S.S—— Thu Dec 20 15:26:38
1990
Received: by well.sf.ca.us (4.12/4.7)
id AA28198; Thu, 20 Dec 90 15:26:32 pst From:
apple!cc.sfu.ca!D. S. S——
Received: from [email address deleted] with SMTP
(5.61/25-eef)
id AA16338; Thu, 20 Dec 90 15:14:19 -0800 for
well.sf.ca.us!bluefire
Received: from [email address deleted] (4.1/1.34) id
AA11940; Thu, 20 Dec 90 15:21:48 PST
Date: Thu, 20 Dec 90 15:11:48 PST

To: [email addresses deleted]
Message-Id: <2741203@cc.sfu.ca>
Subject: FYI Status: R

I received this message via the Progressive
Economists' Network:

From kenbo Mon Dec 17 16:46:00 1990 To: kenbo
Subject: long and scary (and true!) Date: Mon Dec 17
13:42:12 1990

hold onto your shorts folks, george orwell was only
6 years off . . .

I recently forwarded a message about a new Lotus
product—a database on CDROM of 120M US residents
with their estimated incomes and buying profiles.
Someone questioned whether Lotus is really doing
this, so I checked by calling Lotus and speaking to
someone in pre-sales service.

[The long note by Larry Seiler follows.] [12]

In similar fashion, though not as extensively, other notes also began to spread across the Internet. In one example, the author begins by explicitly referring to the nature of this delivery:

```
Fellow e-mail users,
    No, this is not about the war. It is also not
about psi. It is about your privacy, and how it will
be seriously compromised if you do not act. Talk
about an ''electronic wave'' going 'round the
world! . . .
    This message is being passed around the country
via E-mail. The headers on this message included
Maine, UC Santa Barbara, and IBM in Westchester.
I've deleted them for your convenience but the prose
(coming as it does from 10 different authors) is
fractured.[13]
```

The "fractured prose" referred to in this posting is a version of the Seiler letter with other material mixed in. The note also provides readers with a list of items that the author or authors believe are contained in the Lotus database.

Seiler's message and these few others became dominant because they appealed to people's concerns. They were selected from many electronic messages as worthy of being forwarded over and over again until they became representative of the debate. Although the Seiler letter was by far the most prominent, few if any online participants knew Seiler; it was not the person but rather his text that attracted people. The process of circulating this message gave great power to the participants in the online protest, for it allowed them to select a representative message by community consensus and redistribute this message with great reach. This bottom-up process represents one way online rhetorical discourse functions, because the technology promotes such rapid reposting and because the Internet does not have many gatekeeping functions in place. The electronic wave of the MarketPlace protest was thus built by many individuals, not by one individual or group or with an organized plan.

In contrast, the Clipper case involved much more of a top-down structure, and the dominant text in this structure was the petition circulated by CPSR. Well before the Clipper petition, however, the debate over the chip was characterized by professional-sounding postings from such formal bodies as the Clinton administration, the EFF, and CPSR. These postings were well argued, clearly organized, and strategically posted to privacy newsgroups. They were also extremely lengthy. The original announcement from the Clinton administration, for example, took up almost ten computer screens of information (White House 1993). The following excerpt illustrates the question-and-answer format of the posting:

```
QUESTIONS AND ANSWERS ABOUT THE CLINTON
ADMINISTRATION'S TELECOMMUNICATIONS INITIATIVE

Q: Does this approach expand the authority of
government agencies to listen in on phone
conversations?

A: No. ''Clipper Chip'' technology provides law
enforcement with no new authorities to access the
content of the private conversations of Americans.
```

This announcement was followed almost immediately by a posting from CPSR. Entitled "Computer Professionals Call for Public Debate on New Government Encryption Initiative," this message was also well organized, long, and complex. But in spite of the efforts of organizers to spark debate through such messages, the issue of the Clipper chip did not represent the same personal threat to online participants as Lotus MarketPlace. The moderator of one privacy group posted the following comment in response to the lack of initial debate over Clipper:

```
I am surprised that up until this digest no one has
brought up the clipper chip. It is subjects like
that for which this forum was set up.[14]
```

The Clipper debate did inspire a few letters by individuals. Like the Seiler letter in the MarketPlace debate, these letters were reposted across the Internet, appearing on most of the privacy- and Clipper-related newsgroups. On April 17, 1993, the day after the announcement of the Clipper standard, one individual wrote a letter to President Clinton and subsequently posted this letter to the Computer Privacy Digest;[15] another individual wrote a letter to his local senator and posted a copy on the newsgroup alt.security.pgp.[16] Yet these letters were not picked out by other individuals for reposting, as was the Seiler letter during the MarketPlace debate. It was not until December that the Clipper protest became organized, and when it did, the protest centered around postings from the EFF and CPSR.

By December, then, online privacy activists and others on the Internet had heard about Clipper but did not know quite what to do because of the technical complexity of the issue. The CPSR petition, which became the dominant text in the protest, came to represent the attitudes and concerns of participants because it had a built-in process to simplify matters. With the few keystrokes it took to type the phrase "I OPPOSE CLIPPER" and press "send," individuals could sign the petition and feel as if they had done something. The text of the petition, reproduced here in its entirety, included simple instructions for signing (CPSR 1994):

```
Electronic Petition to Oppose Clipper
Please Distribute Widely

On January 24, many of the nation's leading experts
in cryptography and computer security wrote
President Clinton and asked him to withdraw the
Clipper proposal.
    The public response to the letter has been
extremely favorable, including coverage in the New
York Times and numerous computer and security trade
magazines.
    Many people have expressed interest in adding
their names to the letter. In response to these
requests, CPSR is organizing an Internet petition
drive to oppose the Clipper proposal. We will
```

deliver the signed petition to the White House,
complete with the names of all the people who oppose
Clipper.

To sign on to the letter, send a message to:

Clipper.petition@cpsr.org

with the message ''I oppose Clipper'' (no quotes)

You will receive a return message confirming your
vote.

Please distribute this announcement so that
others may also express their opposition to the
Clipper proposal.

CPSR is a membership-based public interest
organization. For membership information, please
email cpsr@cpsr.org. For more information about
Clipper, please consult the CPSR Internet Library—
FTP/WAIS/Gopher CPSR.ORG
/cpsr/privacy/crypto/clipper

==
The President
The White House
Washington, DC 20500
Dear Mr. President:

We are writing to you regarding the ''Clipper''
escrowed encryption proposal now under consideration
by the White House. We wish to express our concern
about this plan and similar technical standards that
may be proposed for the nation's communications
infrastructure.

The current proposal was developed in secret by
federal agencies primarily concerned about
electronic surveillance, not privacy protection.
Critical aspects of the plan remain classified and
thus beyond public review.

The private sector and the public have expressed
nearly unanimous opposition to Clipper. In the

formal request for comments conducted by the
Department of Commerce last year, less than a
handful of respondents supported the plan. Several
hundred opposed it.

If the plan goes forward, commercial firms that
hope to develop new products will face extensive
government obstacles. Cryptographers who wish to
develop new privacy enhancing technologies will be
discouraged. Citizens who anticipate that the
progress of technology will enhance personal privacy
will find their expectations unfulfilled.

Some have proposed that Clipper be adopted on a
voluntary basis and suggest that other technical
approaches will remain viable. The government,
however, exerts enormous influence in the
marketplace, and the likelihood that competing
standards would survive is small. Few in the user
community believe that the proposal would be truly
voluntary.

The Clipper proposal should not be adopted. We
believe that if this proposal and the associated
standards go forward, even on a voluntary basis,
privacy protection will be diminished, innovation
will be slowed, government accountability will be
lessened, and the openness necessary to ensure the
successful development of the nation's
communications infrastructure will be threatened.

We respectfully ask the White House to withdraw
the Clipper proposal.

The Clipper petition was indeed distributed widely. It appeared
on virtually all privacy-, encryption-, and computer-related newsgroups, then quickly spread across the Internet to other newsgroups, lists, and email addresses. The following header accompanied a reposting to PACS-L, an electronic discussion list for
librarians, and points out the reach of the petition's online delivery:

```
From owner-pacs-1@UHUPVM1.UH.EDU Thu Feb 3
08:46:24 1994
Date: Thu, 3 Feb 1994 14:46:24 CST
From: [Greg D——] [email address deleted]
Subject: Re: Petition to Oppose the Clipper Chip
To: Multiple recipients of list PACS-L
<PACS-L@UHUPVM1.bitnet>
----------------Original message----------------
This is an interesting item that has cropped up on
every second list I subscribe to ;-([17]
```

Although the Clipper petition shared a method of delivery with Seiler's letter, it was carefully written and orchestrated by a well-organized lobbying organization. From these two examples of how online texts become dominant, it is clear that more than one model exists for communication in cyberspace. Although both protests involved online delivery, the MarketPlace debate was perhaps more populist in a general sense of the word, while the Clipper debate was somewhat more traditional.

Skipping the Hierarchy

Along with the ways online texts became dominant, two other aspects of structure in the cyberspace protests of MarketPlace and Clipper are worth examining. The first is the how online communication flattens hierarchies, allowing participants to bypass traditional gatekeeping mechanisms and speak directly with those at the top.

Although Seiler's letter and other form letters in the Market-Place protest were motivating to other participants, they required people to make a phone call or write a paper letter. Most online participants in the protest would have preferred to send an email message to Lotus, and this topic arose soon after the debate began in November 1990. One participant, who asked, "Um, does Lotus have an email address to which we can send our request?"[18] did not receive a direct reply, but eventually an email address for Lotus did appear on another online discussion group. This was the address not of the help desk or customer service department but of Jim Manzi, then CEO of Lotus:[19]

> Good People!
> I have received many requests for more information on Lotus' database of information on private US citizens. Here is everything I have received.
> Many people have stated an interest in expressing their opinion of Lotus' database and policies/ attitudes about it. As a community service, here is the email address of Jim Manzi, the CEO of Lotus, for those of you who have something to say to him on the subject.
> Please address your message as follows:
> To: jmanzi@lotus.com[20]

According to one source, email complaints began arriving in Manzi's mailbox, which caused the CEO to become very interested in resolving the MarketPlace problem (former Lotus employee B 1993). Although this method of contacting Manzi directly, bypassing the standard gatekeeping mechanisms of public relations offices, secretaries, and marketing representatives, might also have been attempted with paper letters, these letters would probably have been opened by others within the company. But email went directly into Manzi's personal electronic mailbox.

Three years later, when the Clipper debate began, privacy activists again recognized the power of email and did not hesitate to use it. For example, CPSR organized its petition so that signatures could be collected via a return message; when roughly forty-seven thousand signatures had been collected, CPSR sent the petition to the President. The petition represents both a traditional structure and a new, technologically mediated structure: the method of collecting signatures relied entirely on the process of delivery in cyberspace. In the following posting, Dave Banisar of CPSR prefaced the petition with a comment about how quickly signatures were being collected:

In response the public and private industry has
overwhelmingly opposed the Clipper Proposal. Last
week, many of the nations top cryptographers and
computer security experts, experts on computer
networks, privacy and public interest groups wrote
to the president, asking him to withdraw the
proposal. Many others wanted to in in also. CPSR has
created an internet petition drive. In the first
24 hours, over 1300 people have already signed on.
We ask you to join in.[21]

Participants in the Clipper protest also had the opportunity to
use email to write directly to President Clinton. The president and
other governmental officials had recently obtained email addresses,
and these addresses were soon made available on the privacy discussion groups. One participant, posting the president's email address, suggests that email provides everyone with a chance to "send
positive comments directly as E-Mail, or, if desired, to vent your
spleen without delay!"[22] Yet this participant, citing an article from
the *Washington Post*, also notes that email sent to the president
won't necessarily be read by him:

Just reported today (6/2) on page F3 of The
Washington Post:
    ''Move over 1600 Pennsylvania Avenue, Bill
Clinton has a second address:
president@whitehouse.gov.''
    Several paragraphs later, it reports:
    ''People who send complaints or praise by E-Mail
won't reach the president directly or jump the queue
in getting attention. The messages will be read by
the White House correspondence staff, with the same
priority as paper letters.
    A sampling will be show to the president and Vice
President Al Gore, who made White House E-Mail a
personal priority. (His address:
vice.president@whitehouse.gov).''[23]

Unlike email directed to Lotus's Jim Manzi, then, messages sent to the president would not bypass the gatekeepers. So although both the MarketPlace and Clipper participants used email in attempts to leap past hierarchical communication structures, the organizational features of the two cases were responsible for the effectiveness this process. Lotus's email system did not involve any gatekeeping mechanisms. The White House, however, set up a process by which messages would be screened by staff members. The differences between these two cases once again illustrate the danger and simplicity of ascribing general characteristics to communication and community in cyberspace. The potential for using online communication is clear, but it is ultimately the political and organizational context that dictates how effective such communication will be.

Trust and Anonymity in Online Community

The final structural aspect of these online debates involved a tacit trust in what participants thought of as the Internet community. In both cases, this trust also involved distrust of Big Brother in the form of Lotus or the government. But trust in the Internet community allowed Larry Seiler, who was clearly opposed to having his personal information pressed onto CD-ROM and distributed by Lotus, to feel comfortable posting his home address across the Internet:

```
198 L—— Street
B——, MA——24
December 6, 1990
Lotus Development Corp.
Attn: Market Name Referral Service
55 Cambridge Parkway
Cambridge, MA 02142

Dear Marketeers,
    I do not want my name included in your ''Household
Marketplace'' CDROM database, nor that of anyone in
```

```
my family, at any address I have ever lived at.  To be
specific, please make sure that the following
entries are **NOT** included in your database:
     any last name (especially Seiler, S——, P——, or
Z——) at 198 L——Street, B—— MA
     any Seiler family name at 53 O—— Street, W—— MA
     any Seiler family name at 77 R—— Road, H—— MA²⁵
```

The apparent contradiction in Seiler's letter was noted by a participant in the debate:

```
Interesting that Seiler did not mind his name and
address and a narrow expression of his political
views going on over any network. That's a lot more
telling than a single entry in a CD-ROM.²⁶
```

Another person replied,

```
A telling point . . . which I'd been mulling over. As
we discovered in the Journalists' topic, there's a
perceived community implicit in an electronic
network (even a broad one like the Internet) that
does not exist in a mere mailing list. Part of it is
the cultural tradition of mutual respect which has
emerged over most conferencing systems.²⁷
```

This "cultural tradition" extended to the text of Seiler's letter, which contained an overt expression of his faith in the Internet community:

```
In interviews, Lotus has said that individuals will
NOT be able to correct their own entries, or even
see what they are. I didn't try to confirm this in my
call to Lotus, but I did confirm that the person who
reported it—R—— S—— of [company name deleted]—has
an excellent reputation on the internet. Also,
everything he said that I checked with Lotus is
absolutely accurate. Further, the Wall Street
Journal has reported on it—saying that the database
```

has ages, marital status, and other such personal
data as well.[28]

This tacit sense of trust in a perceived community was a large part of what made the Lotus protest successful. The Seiler letter was spread with little concern that his information came from someone with no connection to Lotus Corporation but rather from someone with an "excellent reputation on the internet."

In both the MarketPlace and Clipper cases, postings did not even need an author's name to inspire this trust and be reposted. Anonymous postings were also provided as a kind of community service, although they were not explicitly stated as such. The anonymous posting that was supposedly an internal memo from Lotus Corporation, which circulated at the end of the MarketPlace debate, is one example. In the Clipper protest, a similar kind of trust was evident in the mass reposting of the anonymous message containing detailed financial and other corporate information about Mykotronx, the company chosen to be the primary manufacturer of the chip:

Here are excerpts of the general ledger of
Mykotronx, the Torrance Based Big-Brother outfit
that is going to make the Clinton Clipper wiretap
chip. I have left off their chart of accounts
numbers, since you don't care about that. Do not
reveal the source of this document (me) to anyone.[29]

The author of the posting had used simple Internet tools to allow the origin of the posting to remain hidden. Yet the information was widely accepted as true by people who trusted the Internet privacy community. Even though the author was anonymous, the figures contained in the posting (excerpted below) were widely circulated.

1.	Preliminary Studies	$268,074	2/14/92
2.	Place Subcontract w/VLSI	$47,917	2/22/92
3.	Complete PDR KG-44B	$61,431	4/13/92
4.	Complete PDR VLSI	$71,090	5/19/92
5.	Complete SFA Review VLSI	$78,470	7/12/92

6.	Complete CDR VLSI	$106,638	7/17/92
7.	Complete first KG-44B	$166,641	8/12/92
8.	Complete CDR	$132,454	6/18/92
9.	Complete tests 1st KG-48B	$151,957	12/16/92
10.	Complete fab VLSI	$203,941	11/17/92

Confidence in members of the online privacy community, then, was a critical factor in the structure of the MarketPlace and Clipper protests. This sense of trust leads us to the next critical issue: accountability and accuracy in cyberspace. Why, for example, are certain texts selected as trustworthy? Why is there such trust in an invisible or nonphysical community? Do speed, anonymity, and a strong ethos promote inaccurate information and hyperbolic language? In an analysis of the protests, these questions become central.

6 Ethos, Flaming, and Inaccuracy

Many individuals on the Internet, especially those concerned with privacy and free speech, have traditionally held a kind of libertarian viewpoint emphasizing self-governance of information. As is obvious from their distrust of Big Brother, these individuals are against most forms of gatekeeping in cyberspace and instead rely on what they see as the self-regulating mechanism of the net community to weed out false or unwarranted information. The trust that Seiler (and others who subsequently reposted his message) placed in someone who had an "excellent reputation on the Internet" is an example of this faith in information gleaned from cyberspace. Many participants hope this tacit sense of trust will be the basis for the future of cyberspace, because, they believe, it allows individuals to voice their opinions and share information freely. They assume that this open discussion will somehow lead to "the truth." Indeed, observers have looked to cyberspace as potentially revitalizing to democracy and participatory debate, a concept with which many of the participants in the MarketPlace and Clipper debates would no doubt agree.

Yet this model relies heavily on the notion that debate in cyberspace is devoid of features other than the factual information contained in electronic messages; the model ignores the power of ethos in rhetorical discourse.[1] When we hear or read a message, we do not choose to believe it based solely on its content. Indeed, the content of any message is inherently interwoven with a certain character, or ethos, and this ethos is a powerful determinant of whether speakers and their messages are accepted by the audience. The character and credibility of the speaker are often considered the most important features in rhetoric, because if audiences do not trust a speaker, they will probably not listen to his or her message. People reposted the Seiler letter as widely as they did not simply because the technology allowed them to do so or because the information contained in the letter appeared important or truthful, but also because something about the letter resonated with them, appealed to them, or made them believe Seiler's arguments. Similarly, it was not the individual letters to the president that were widely distributed during the Clipper chip protest. Instead, it was CPSR's electronic petition, which offered not only the content but also the appropriate character and credibility to appeal to privacy advocates and other participants across the Internet.

The dominance of certain texts in the debates illustrates the power of ethos in cyberspace and complicates the liberal model of online community by illustrating that "truth" does not always prevail, especially in the highly specialized spaces of the Internet. In any community of shared values, including the discretely divided electronic communities of newsgroups, mailing lists, and other cyberspaces, the model of free discussion is often composed of Athenians being praised in Athens. The MarketPlace and Clipper cases show that communities often become self-selecting and may not challenge the information they obtain in cyberspace forums. Instead, they choose to believe it because certain messages appeal to their shared values. The ability to rapidly edit and repost information heightens this process, so that messages with strong appeal may be reposted widely with little critical review of the informational content. The current structure of the Internet is thus the classic double-edged sword: while it allows for many people to connect with each other across space and time, it may also, especially in the discrete communities of Usenet newsgroups and discussion lists, promote insularity and offer fertile ground for unchecked information.

Ethos and Inaccuracy in Cyberspace

The debate over Lotus MarketPlace contained highly emotive and angry statements, which at times included and seemed to encourage the spread of inaccurate or exaggerated information about MarketPlace. With no one person or group in charge of checking the contents of postings, it was up to readers to determine the accuracy of the messages they were reading. Yet many participants had a sense of trust in the credibility of Internet information and the Internet community. As the protest grew, and as notes were appended and reposted, the information circulated about Market-Place was often exaggerated or even untrue. Therefore, what resulted was, on the one hand, an open debate, a bottom-up protest, and a new type of citizen action. But, on the other hand, this debate involved a highly emotive ethos and much inaccurate information.

The ethos of the Seiler letter, for example, is evident in its sarcastic salutation "Dear Marketeers" and in its concluding paragraph. In addition, throughout the letter, personal and angry language illustrates Seiler's hostility and deep distrust of Lotus Corporation:

> As you have it set up, I think your ''Household
> Marketplace'' CDROM database is an incredible
> intrusion and ought to be illegal. I am a computer
> professional, so this opinion is not based on any
> native dislike of computers or databases. The
> problems I have with your proposed service involve
> the way in which you plan to administer it, the way
> in which the data will almost certainly be used, the
> type of data you are including, and my conviction
> that you will vigorously seek to avoid
> responsibility for errors in your database.
>
> First, administration. I have heard that you are
> not providing any means to correct errors in your
> database. The potential for long term damage to
> individuals from use of your database is therefore
> enormous. Even if an individual knows that your
> database is false, users of your database will
> almost certainly believe the CDROM data in spite of
> any disclaimers or evidence offered by the
> individual.
>
> Second, use of data. Given the fact that law
> enforcement agencies are nearly powerless to shut
> down obviously illegal boiler-room businesses, it is

absurd for you to claim that you will only provide
the data to legitimate businesses. You won't be able
to prevent your product from being used to defraud
individuals by huge numbers of illegal operations.
One way or another, essentially any business who
wants your database will be able to get it—and it
will be of special value to illegal and borderline
businesses.

   Third, type of data. I understand that you plan to
publish ''income estimates.'' There is no legal way
for you to verify income, unless an individual
voluntarily provides that information. (I never do,
except when the data is legally required to be held
in confidence.) It is absolutely unacceptable for
you to publish what amount to rumors about people's
income. The possibilities for abuse are enormous.

   Fourth, responsibility. I understand that you
will not permit individuals to find out what
information you are spreading about them. The only
likely reason for this is that you don't want anyone
to find out that your information about them is
false. Therefore, while you will sell this product
on the basis of providing reliable information, you
aren't prepared to be responsible for the accuracy
of your information, or for the damage that false
information (or even true information) might cause.

   So as you see, my concerns about your product are
not primarily about privacy, although privacy is
involved. If you were prepared to take responsibility for the accuracy of your information, then
I would be willing to accept your service. For
example, you could send copies of the data entries
to *each* individual in your database, with a
request to write back if any of the data is
incorrect or if they want to be removed from your
listing. If you did this, and *made* the requested

```
corrections, then I would feel that you were
providing a positive service, rather than making
abusive use of unverified data.
     In conclusion, if you market this product, it is
my sincere hope that you are sued by every person
for whom your data is false, with the eventual
result that your company goes bankrupt. That would
be a pity, since you make many fine products.
However, that is preferable to permitting you to
spread rumors and encourage abusive business
practices. It would be better if your chief officers
went to jail, but that will apparently require new
laws to be passed. If you persist in your plans to
market this product, a lot of people will be pushing
to make that happen. I suggest that you abandon this
project while there is time to do so.²
```

This extreme and angry style has come to be known on computer networks as "flaming," which has been defined as "the hostile expression of strong emotions and feelings" (Lea et al. 1992, 89).³ In the Lotus case, this angry ethos played an important role in maintaining the protest community and the ensuing debate. Flaming is common in cyberspace, and such language appealed to the community not only because of its style but also because it openly expressed the personal sentiments of those who opposed the product. Participants in the MarketPlace debate felt directly threatened by the product. And Seiler's use of flaming combined with his personal sense of anger created an effective ethos to appeal to others in the privacy communities of the Internet.

A second posting, which was also widely circulated during the Lotus debate, lacks overt hostility but still uses extreme language:

```
Summary: Basically, Lotus is putting together a
database, about to be released on CD-rom in March.
It will contain a LOT of personal information about
YOU, which anyone in the country can access by just
```

buying the discs. It seems to me (and a lot of other
people, too) that this will be a little too much of a
big brother, and it seems like a good idea to get out
while there is still time. Feel free to forward this
message to as many people as you know.

A similar tone is also apparent in the same letter's last paragraph:

I can even imagine commercial espionage, where the
Lotus database was somehow ''stolen,'' and bootleg
copies of the database were then offered on the
''black market.'' I shudder to think of all of this
combined information available for the asking, IN
ONE PLACE.[4]

Although the reference to Big Brother may accurately characterize this participant's feelings about MarketPlace and some aspects
of the product, it also conveys a sense of caution and outrage to
the readers. In the same fashion, the idea that the database might
be copied and distributed without Lotus's consent is technically
possible, but such language as "black market" adds a heightened
sense of concern to this suggestion.

In addition to an angry tone, which can certainly be argued to
be a valid response to the announcement of MarketPlace, these letters also tended to include inaccurate information. Seiler's letter,
for example, states the following:

Second, pass this message along to anyone whom you
think might care. To me, this is not just a matter of
privacy. Lotus is going to sell information behind
our backs—we are not allowed to dispute their data
or even know what it is. Worse, Lotus is going to
sell rumors about our income. Still worse, they will
do it on a scale never before achieved. This should
not be tolerated. Please help to stop Lotus.[5]

Lotus was not selling rumors about people's incomes. Rather,
the company had obtained information about income ranges from

the credit company Equifax and had incorporated this information into the database. Furthermore, it is questionable whether Lotus MarketPlace would spread this information "on a scale never before achieved." Although the product did have serious privacy implications, the scale of distribution would probably not have exceeded the everyday distribution of information by such companies as Equifax or TRW. Because Seiler's information came not from Lotus itself but rather from sources within the online privacy community, the letter is not completely accurate. The appeal of its ethos, however, was more powerful to online participants than was the desire to verify its information. Seiler himself admitted that he checked his "facts" not with Lotus but rather with a person who was trusted within the Internet community.

A more detailed and striking example of inaccuracy is illustrated in the following passage from the other dominant posting:

```
Lotus ''Household Marketplace'':
In one one database, the combined knowledge may
include such things that we normally expect to
consider private:

o family members' names, gender, and ages (!)
o address and home phone number
o annual salary
o debt-to-earnings ratio
o net worth (house, cars, misc. household items)
o investment portfolio (stocks, CD's, etc.)
o self and spouse employer info
o health and life insurance plan info
o schools attended by my children
o kind of car(s) I own              }
o kind of computer I own            } from
o kind of stereo equipment I own    } ''warranty''
o kind of video equipment I own     } registrations
o kind of household appliances I own }
o who knows what else?[6]
```

This list is an exaggerated and inaccurate account of Market-
Place. Most of the items on the list, such as kind of car or computer owned, were not included in the Lotus database. Even items
that were included are reported inaccurately here; for example,
this list says "annual salary" when what MarketPlace actually contained was a salary range for each household. Furthermore, none of
the MarketPlace data came directly from warranty cards (although
the data provided by Equifax may at one time have been compiled based on warranty information). Nonetheless, the author or
authors of the above list were under no obligation to check sources.
The message had grown in each reposting in a way reminiscent of
the party game where people sit in a circle, someone whispers a
phrase, the phrase is passed around the circle in whispers, and the
last person says aloud the phrase he or she heard, which by then
is a totally different phrase. What had resulted in the case of the
Lotus message was the preceding list. The bottom-up structure of
this protest, so conducive to individual participation and open debate, is thus highly susceptible to the intrusion of inaccuracies,
which, given the rapidity of online delivery, can easily become com-
pounded with each new posting.

Both the hostile language and exaggerated and inaccurate information were critical in the appeal of the two MarketPlace-related
postings, and within weeks, both messages had wide circulation
and had become dominant in the MarketPlace debate. Despite
their inaccurate information, these postings resonated with others
on the Internet; subsequently, the online protest soon had generated more than thirty thousand complaints to Lotus Development
Corporation.

In the protest over the Clipper chip, the ethos was, unlike that of
the MarketPlace debate, generally one of professionalism and technical accuracy. The petition written and organized by CPSR was
carefully crafted in a style appropriate for correspondence with the
White House. Recognizing that highly emotive letters like Seiler's
would not be effective for addressing the president of the United
States, CPSR produced a letter that sounded official and well researched. The contrast between the two letters is evident as early

as the salutation. The Clipper letter is straightforwardly headed "Dear Mr. President" and opens with a formal paragraph stating the reason for the letter and the misgivings over the Clipper EES proposal. After a detailed listing of these concerns, the letter ends by indicating that the signers "respectfully ask the White House to withdraw the Clipper proposal." The body of the letter (see Chapter 5) is also formal and respectful, politely indicating that the authors "wish to express [their] concern." The professional style of the letter conveyed an ethos of respectability and serious-ness. Combined with CPSR's credibility as an organization and its strong presence in the privacy newsgroups and lists, this style pro-duced an ethos that was appealing to cyberspace participants. The final paragraph of the Clipper petition summarizes the reasons why Clipper should not be adopted, noting that

```
privacy protection will be diminished, innovation
will be slowed, government accountability will be
lessened, and the openness necessary to ensure the
successful development of the nation's communica-
tions infrastructure will be threatened.
```

These possible outcomes did not inspire the personal outrage that the Seiler letter did. Furthermore, the technical complexities of Clipper made it hard for people (except for those who special-ized in encryption or followed the debate closely) to grasp what the threat of Clipper would be, so information was circulated mainly by experts and thus stayed reasonably accurate. But participants across the Internet respected CPSR, and based on what they knew of Clipper, they used the immediate mechanism of sending an email message to add their name to the letter. The forty-seven thou-sand or more signatures garnered in the anti-Clipper campaign were due to the strong ethos of CPSR's petition.

Community, Ethos, and Dominance

The previous analysis illustrates that in each case, ethos was a powerful factor in how specific texts became dominant. This analysis proves that both the bottom-up model of MarketPlace and the top-down model of Clipper were effective in allowing individuals to voice their opinions and take action. As certain texts circulated across the Internet, communities of action and protest sprang up in response. Special newsgroups and discussion lists were quickly put into place, and the spaces already devoted to computers and privacy were focused to a large extent around the concerns over both products. On the face of it, this scenario bodes well for the libertarian model of cyberspace. Even though CPSR's text was orchestrated from the top down, it was still distributed by many individuals on the Internet. In both cases, it appears that individuals formed communities that used these forums for open debate.

Yet the power of ethos and dominance in online communities is a potential problem. Communities are inclined to believe what already appeals to their values; this inclination is especially apparent in the MarketPlace postings, where inaccurate information was not challenged. When some participants attempted to raise this issue, they were not readily welcomed into the debate. In fact, their views were often snubbed. Toward the end of the MarketPlace protest, for example, a contributor to the Telecom Privacy Digest challenged the information in many of the postings, noting that in his opinion, most of what he had seen on the network constituted "pure lies":

> Most of the postings I saw in various news groups opposing the product asserted pure lies about the content of the data base. . . .
> With the exception of the mailing address, the proposed data was demographic, not personal.[7]

Although it is questionable whether "most" (in the quantitative sense) of the postings contained inaccuracies, this participant is no doubt commenting on the general ethos he experienced from the dominant postings, an ethos that was composed in large part of hyperbolic statements and inaccurate information.

All participants in the MarketPlace protest appeared to have the capability of voicing their opinions, but consent was the norm within most of the conferences. Most participants agreed that Lotus MarketPlace was a serious deviation from other direct mail efforts and was thus a privacy threat. When lone individuals did not think MarketPlace was a problem, their opinions were quickly dismissed by others. In the Telecom Privacy Digest, for example, the moderator started a short-lived thread with the subject line "Much Ado About Nothing." After reading a long anti-MarketPlace note (containing the Seiler letter, among other material), the digest's moderator posted a reply beginning as follows:

```
Date: Sun, 30 Dec 90 11:53:42 CST
From: TELECOM Moderator [email address deleted]
Subject: Much Ado About Nothing

In this issue of TELECOM Digest, I've included a
greatly edited file I received discussing the plans
of Lotus to market a national database of names,
addresses, telephone numbers and other details. The
opinion of the submitter was that this is going to
be a terrible invasion of privacy, and a source of
much incorrect information, leading to trouble for
the individuals in the data base. I don't think this
is the case at all.
    We've heard news in recent weeks about another
national, computerized and publicly accessible
database of telephone numbers and addresses: the one
offered by Compuserve (GO PHONEFILE) to anyone who
wants to pay a $15 per hour surcharge to use it in
addition to normal Compuserve rates.
    The only thing different about the CIS program and
the proposed Lotus program—the only break with the
past—is that these are a little easier and more
convenient to use. The information has always been
there. Criss-cross directories, listing precisely
the same information, have been around since before
this century. Credit bureaus have had the
information for just as long: the first credit
```

bureau in this country started in the middle 1800s.
There have been *regional* databases for many years
containing all this information.

   You cannot place information about yourself in
the public record and then object when someone
gathers it all together in a convenient, easy for
the public to read style. My home telephone numbers
are non-pub. I have yet to see them in any criss-
cross—electronic or paper—anywhere. Why should Lotus
and/or Compuserve be castigated on this net any more
or less than the Haines Publishing Company? Why
should credit bureaus keep records and Lotus not
keep records?[8]

This message generated a series of responses, most of which were
in disagreement with this idea. In the same issue of the digest,
for example, another participant commented, "With all due respect, it's somewhat cavalier to call the issues raised by this product 'nothing.'"[9] This participant continued in a lengthy note to
debate Patrick Townson's opinion about MarketPlace. The discussion continued through many issues of the digest, with most of
the subsequent notes disagreeing with Townson and arguing that
Lotus MarketPlace was indeed a privacy problem, as in the following posting.

Date: Mon, 31 Dec 90 08:10:06 -0800
From: [Seth J. R——] [email address deleted]
Subject: Re: Much Ado About Nothing

[forwarded by the Telecom moderator]

In article [email address deleted] (TELECOM
Moderator) writes:

> The opinion
> of the submitter was that this is going to be a
> terrible invasion of
> privacy, and a source of much incorrect
> information, leading to

```
> trouble for the individuals in the data base. I
> don't think this is
> the case at all.
```

I disagree. And the reason is not so much that LOTUS
will be publishing the data, but that there is no
way for the consumer to verify that the data are
accurate or current, or to register a ''difference
of opinion.''[10]

This note continues at length, excerpting from the original "Much Ado" note and commenting on each section. Many other similar notes followed; on another list, one participant noted that the issue of mailing list sales "has long been moot,"[11] but his point was quickly refuted by others, and it never received much discussion, even though it was true that much of the data on the Lotus disc was already available. But these individual attempts at viewing the problem from another perspective did not have the powerful ethos of the Seiler letter, and they were never cross-posted beyond their original discussion groups. The bottom-up style of participation in the MarketPlace protest thus involved closed communities, whose trust in the community ethos often ruled out open debate in favor of a belief in widely circulated but inaccurate information.

The top-down model of the Clipper case, while it did provide for more accurate information, may in its own way have stifled conversation and encouraged an insider attitude toward the protest. Like the MarketPlace messages, CPSR's anti-Clipper petition was powerful in its ability to reach many people. It also had the added feature of allowing participants to sign on by simply sending a return email message to CPSR. Yet, as some online activists noted, the strong ethos of a professional organization can easily discourage individuals from seeking outside information.

The moderator of the Privacy Forum Digest addressed this issue directly. After first noting the highly emotional tone of the latest Clipper-related submissions to the digest (which he characterized as "replete with ad hominem attacks and emotionally potent but logically deprived arguments"), he expressed his concern about the dominance of the CPSR petition, because of both delivery issues (the ability of a single individual to send in more than one signature) and the strong ethos of CPSR:

> Other activities regarding this debate are also
> of concern. As you may know, CPSR (Computer
> Professionals for Social Responsibility) has been
> sponsoring an e-mail anti-Clipper petition drive.
> EFF (Electronic Frontier Foundation) is sponsoring
> a similar e-mail based drive to pressure for U.S.
> Congressional hearings regarding Clipper.
>
> While many of the goals of both organizations
> are often laudable, I am not convinced that such
> ''petition'' techniques are appropriate to the
> circumstances at hand. The ease of sending e-mail
> means that it would probably be possible to get 10s
> of 1000s of quickie ''add my name to the list''
> messages to such automated petition servers for
> virtually *any* topic. People don't have to
> understand, think about, or even have really heard
> about a subject, they just shoot an empty message
> off to an address and add their userid to the list.
> Even if we assume that there isn't much fraud from
> persons sending in multiple messages under differing
> names (certainly possible and simple on many
> systems) what does such quickie knee-jerk response
> mechanisms provide to enhance the debate?
>
> CPSR has been comparing the response to their
> current drive to the similar effort conducted
> against ''Lotus Marketplace'' sometime back. One
> could argue that the techniques used to convince a
> private firm not to market a particular niche
> information product (and of course, all the related
> information is still widely available!) is not
> necessarily applicable to arguing against a major
> cryptographic system with strong government backing

and apparently not inconsiderable bipartisan support
(at least outside of the ''technical'' community).
CPSR has also recently been ''promoting'' a ''Big
Brother Inside'' postscript picture that I feel
serves little but to further trivialize this matter.

Such ''power by numbers'' petitions remind me of
the efforts (sometimes successful) of various
pressure groups to force advertisers to drop support
of television programs with aspects that the
particular group finds distasteful, and of the
practice of some radio talk show hosts to encourage
their listeners to flood some entity with calls
and/or letters opposing or supporting particular
views. In almost all of these cases, the key isn't
reasoned debate, it's just names and numbers—to try
blind them with shear volume!

That such techniques are sometimes successful,
and that politicians and organizations will often
react to such pressure petition drives, should not
be an endorsement of such techniques being used.
There is more at stake than simply ''winning'' a
particular argument—the general coarsening of debate
on so many topics into a flurry of opinion polls,
petition drives, emotional television images, and
the briefest of soundbites, threatens to change the
nature of democracy in fundamental and negative
ways. . . .

Please folks. I know it's easy to get wound up in
these matters—all the more so when it's so simple to
just shoot off an e-mail message in a matter of
minutes. But unless we all try to take the high road
in these discussions, the importance of the issues
are going to be drowned out in the shouting. Then,
ultimately, we *all* lose, on both sides of the
debate.[12]

In a later issue of the digest, the moderator again takes up this concern, noting that in his opinion, many people who held the outsider opinion of favoring Clipper were in fact afraid of making this opinion known on the privacy forums of the Internet:

> My point was that it's important to keep in mind that there are more people supporting Clipper than one might imagine from reading on the network. I've received notes from people expressing their fear of making ''politically incorrect'' statements on the net by saying something publicly that might be viewed as ''pro-Clipper.'' I believe that anti-Clipper efforts predicated on the assumption that there's no significant support for Clipper might be weakening their own effectiveness.

He then returns to the discussion of CPSR's petition, suggesting that many of the people who signed it via email may not, in fact, have done any additional research beyond reading the content of the petition itself.

> As several people have pointed out, CPSR has a wealth of detailed arguments regarding Clipper available. However, it would be interesting to know what percentage of persons responding to the petition did so immediately after reading it and based only on the material they read in the petition itself.
>
> With a sufficiently large population and a well-worded document it might be possible to get 10s of 1000s of persons to sign-on to most any topic. I suspect that e-mail petition drives will end up being viewed as the electronic equivalent of form letter writing campaigns—which are nothing new to commercial firms and government entities alike. Such campaigns are not, in *my opinion*, the best way to

```
deal with complex topics, but of course it is
everyone's right to participate in them.¹³
```

The thread of this discussion was picked up by Marc Rotenberg of CPSR, who responded with a well-crafted and carefully articulated posting. Recognizing at the outset that "just as the proponents of Clipper speak too frequently of terrorists and pedaphiles, opponents must be careful not to ring the Big Brother alarms too quickly," he continued with his arguments against Clipper and in favor of the CPSR petition:

```
CPSR strongly supports informed public debate
on cryptography policy. In fact, that has been
virtually our watchword since we first testified in
Congress five years ago on the implementation of the
Computer Security Act and warned that NSA's
encroachment into standard setting for civilian
computer systems would have serious consequences for
the public use of cryptography and privacy
protection for network users. We called for open
hearings then and have pushed the issue at every
opportunity since.

    Since that hearing, CPSR has also organized three
cryptography policy conferences in Washington,
litigated more than half a dozen Freedom of
Information Act cases, appeared before numerous
government panels to discuss cryptography policy,
and made a wide range of policy documents available
to the public through CPSR.ORG.

    Our conferences have included representatives
from the NSA, the FBI, the Department of Justice,
and the White House. Documents obtained from CPSR
FOIA requests have been reported on in national
papers, and copies of CPSR cryptography resource
books may be found in the offices of members of
Congress and the White House.
```

We have been uncompromising in our commitment to an open, fair, thoughtful debate on cryptography policy.

The CPSR Clipper petition grows out of a five-year history of litigation, testimony, reporting, analysis, and assessment involving cryptography issues. . . .

After the White House announcement in early February of the plan to go forward with Clipper and in response to requests we received from many people who wanted to add their names to the original letter, we decided to circulate the petition on the network and encourage signatures.

We did not expect the response we received. The Marketplace campaign generated 30,000 email messages over a six month period. It was highly publicized and well focused. The current debate about the Clipper proposal has been clouded by other related but less significant issues.

Nonetheless, the total number of people who signed the CPSR Clipper petition recently topped 25,000 and the number continues to grow.

While I am sympathetic to Lauren's concerns about the possible misuse of the network to rally support for a particular political viewpoint, I think he would be a hard-pressed to find a similar petition that reflects more careful research, that is as strongly supported by those most knowledgeable about the problem or is more timely. . . .

The political calculation inside the White House is that they can ''give'' this issue to the NSA, and ride out the mild storm of criticism because not enough people understand the Clipper issue and not enough people will actually speak out publicly.

That is why we need people to sign the petition.

> To send a clear, unambigous message to the White
> House that Clipper is a mistake and should be
> withdrawn.
>
> That is why we ask you to support our efforts.[14]

This message is clear, reasoned, and well argued. It reflects the professional and technically accurate ethos of CPSR. Yet this reply does not address the question of ethos and dominance; that is, it does not state how much research those who signed the petition conducted, beyond simply reading the first few lines. Although Rotenberg notes that more than twenty-five thousand signatures had been appended to the petition at that time, his message does not address Lauren Weinstein's concern that one person could have signed the petition more than once and therefore that CPSR's figure was hard to interpret.

Another participant took up the discussion, commenting on his reluctance to express opinions that dissented from the predominant community position and on what he viewed as the "contradictory beliefs" of community in cyberspace:

> Bravo! I've watched, with much distress, the
> extremely low level of debate on this whole
> issue. . . .
>
> I've made one or two contributions here and there
> that were not seen as ''politically correct,'' but I
> must say I've been reluctant to get involved. The
> level of vituperation in the attacks against Dorothy
> Denning everywhere, and against David Sternlight in
> the cryptography newsgroup—both at complete odds
> with the reasoned and often quite reasonable things
> they have to say—are hardly encouraging. A threat of
> a lawsuit as a response to one message I sent to CuD
> is hardly more so.
>
> My personal feeling is that the end result of all
> the ranting and raving will be to render any
> reasonable opposition to a number of government
> actions on cryptography and privacy ineffective—it's

```
*so* easy to tar someone with a ''nut case radical''
label. People writing on the Internet seem to hold a
couple of contradictory beliefs: (a) If everyone
here agrees with me, *everyone* agrees with me;
(b) What I say here is ''among friends,'' and won't
be seen by ''the bad guys''—i.e., the non-agreeing
members of Congress and so on; (c) the Net can
influence the real world. In fact, (a) has never had
much of any connection with reality, (b) was true
but is rapidly becoming false, and (c) was false but
is rapidly becoming true. And look how we of the net
are presenting ourselves in our first major
political contest.
     Depressing.[15]
```

Another participant also agreed about what he called the "dangers of electronic petitions" and recommended that people think more closely about the "benefits of careful deliberation on complex issues."[16] He and others with similar opinions were recognizing the power of an online ethos and the tendency for people on the Internet to react quickly without weighing all sides of an issue. But in some of these discussions, there was no "other side" to be weighed, because individuals who held the minority position were not comfortable challenging the dominant ethos of the privacy community.

A Critical Eye toward Cyberspace

Although the notion of cyberspace as an egalitarian place where individuals engage in open and free debate is inviting, especially given the speed and power of online delivery, this concept should be viewed with a critical eye. The protests over MarketPlace and Clipper were based on a tacit trust in the Internet community, whose ethos reinforced the spread of inaccurate information and discouraged dissenting opinions. In fact, this ethos also involved an explicitly gendered tone.

7 Gender in Cyberspace

The strong sense of gender inequity that is becoming apparent on the Internet is another challenge to the notion of cyberspace communities as free and open forums. Like the dominant ethos analyzed in the previous chapter, this inequity presses at the concept of the vox populi and freedom of expression, supporting instead the claim that cyberspace reflects and perhaps even intensifies the gender inequities and biases already existing in the world. The current myths of cyberspace involve the libertarian notion that all parties have equal access to discussion and conversation; that somehow, discussions in the virtual forum are judged solely on their content and not on the ethos of the posting or the social judgments of the readers. A typical thought along these lines is expressed in the following excerpt from an article in *Computer-Mediated Communication Magazine:*

> On the Net anyone has the freedom to say anything they want, within the very broad confines of libel laws, self-censorship, and liberal community norms. The only insurmountable restriction on freedom of speech in cyberspace is that conversation must remain within the prescribed topic of any given online conference. Anyone can say anything they want but they must say it in the designated forum for the subject. (Strangelove 1994)

Even a ten-year-old child, writing in the *Utne Reader*, commented on this sense of freedom: "One of the greatest things about the Internet is that no one has to know who you are . . . if you are on the Internet, things like age are unimportant—or invisible, anyway, if you want them to be" (Kearney 1995).

Early research on computer-mediated communication offered some support for the notion that the technology might allow women, who traditionally do not speak up as often or with as much

"On the Internet, nobody knows you're a dog."

Figure 7.1. This now famous cartoon suggests the ability of online participants to mask or change gender (or even species) in cyberspace. Drawing by P. Steiner; copyright © 1993 The New Yorker Magazine, Inc. Reprinted by permission.

vigor as men, to participate more equally in online conversations. This research includes descriptions of more equal participation in group decision making generally (Siegel et al. 1986) and specific examples of women students who spoke up more frequently in on-line chat sessions than in the physical classroom (Faigley 1992). Yet a close look at the MarketPlace and Clipper cases indicates that most participants were men; in the rare cases when women did participate, their voices were often marked by a decidedly different style and level of acceptance in the protest communities. Observers with an interest in gender on the Internet have recently begun to speculate on a number of possible reasons for these differences in number and tone.

Women and Access to Computing Technology

In both protests, far fewer women than men participated.[1] In the MarketPlace protest, more than half the participants were male; in the highly technical Clipper debates, this bias is even more obvious, as only a few women ventured into the discussions. The most obvious reason for this inequity is the issue of access. Historically, computer science has been a field dominated by men, a trend that may change over time but is still very real in the world of high-technology research and development. Because the Internet was originally inhabited primarily by these male computer scientists (including students), women's presence in cyberspace has traditionally been limited. In addition, women occupy lower socioeconomic levels in the United States and worldwide, and they have less access to computers and modems than do men. Although this trend may be shifting with the introduction of commercial online services and lower-priced hardware, surveys indicate that "cyberspace remains a masculine environment" (Covert 1995).

This "masculine environment" is based not only on issues of access to equipment but also on issues of access to the content of discussions. Once women are connected to the Internet, the highly technical nature of many online discussions continues to make cyberspace even more exclusive. Because the Internet was originally set up by men in science and technology, it has retained the technical discussions that have traditionally excluded women. Even though much time had passed since the initial development of the Internet and its sexist overtones (fig. 7.2), the MarketPlace discussion appeared to involve far more men than women. Yet MarketPlace had a personal appeal ("my name and address on a CD-ROM") and thus was of interest to some women; in the Clipper case, by contrast, hardly any women's names appear, in large part because cryptology, combining mathematics and computer science, is a male-dominated field.

"When mental models are dissimilar, the achievement of communication
might be signaled by changes in the structure of one of the models—or both of them"

Figure 7.2. A cartoon from one of the original articles by the founders of the
early Internet (then called ARPANET). The article (written in 1968) was
extremely forward-thinking in its speculation about online communities, but
its use of cartoons like this one (in a section describing how computer models
must match the user's mental models) indicates that sexism was part of the
technology from the beginning. See Licklider, Taylor, and Herbert 1968.

Oddly, given this fact, one of the most prominent voices in the
Clipper debate was also one of the few women in the discussion.
Professor Dorothy Denning, chair of the computer science department at Georgetown University, is a cryptography expert and the
author of one of the canonical texts on the subject. Yet Denning
was ostracized from the beginning of the protest. Her involvement
in the Clipper debate and the way she was subsequently treated by
the online activists is worth a closer look, because what happened
to Denning suggests that even when women are highly credentialed
and have the technical skill for certain Internet discussions, they
can be subject to misogynist attitudes in cyberspace.

Witches, Outsiders, and Cyberspace

Dorothy Denning's role in the Clipper case began with her book
Cryptography and Data Security, written in 1983, which established

her as an expert in the field of cryptography. Even though she is highly credentialed, Denning was destined to become an outsider in the cyberspace communities for two reasons: first, because she agreed with the design of and need for Clipper, thus siding with Big Brother; and second, because she is a woman. Denning was one of a number of experts asked by the NSA to analyze the Clipper chip for any flaws or potential ability to be "cracked" or "hacked" by an outsider. Prior to her dealings with Clipper, Denning had acted as an expert witness in other government cases; in 1990, her testimony "demolished" the prosecution's case against a college student who had published material on the Internet (Hotz 1993). In the case of Clipper and EES, Denning, after analyzing the standard, believed Clipper could not be cracked. Furthermore, she was in favor of the government having a secure encryption standard for legal use, and her viewpoints were widely broadcast in the print media as well as in cyberspace. She posted frequent messages to the Internet; many were highly technical and contained her carefully constructed arguments in favor of Clipper.

Responses to Denning's opinions about Clipper and to her presence in the debate were characterized by a misogynist ethos.[2] The most obvious example of this ethos was a series of postings, which soon took on a life of their own, referring to Denning as the Wicked Witch of the East. Historically, of course, witches were women who lived a lifestyle that was threatening to mainstream political and religious communities, and they were ultimately burned at the stake for their opinions and practices. It is no wonder, then, that Denning was "flamed" for her viewpoints; one participant indicated that her opinions were "part of a continuing propaganda campaign to marginalize and demonize advocates of electronic privacy rights."[3] This ethos was heightened by online delivery, as the "wicked witch" thread spread across many newsgroups and discussion lists, ultimately catching the attention of mainstream journalists (Hotz 1993). In addition, many participants referred to Denning as "Ms. Denning" (rather than as "Dr." or "Professor"), which diminished her credibility and sounded patronizing and smug. Although participants were most adamant about her associations with the NSA (calling her a "mouthpiece for the NSA's anti-privacy party line"),[4] their outrage was often expressed in terms of Denning's gender, not just her viewpoint.

In fairness, not all the participants in the Clipper debate were so overtly sexist and juvenile. One participant, in a posting with the subject line "emotion vs. reason in the Clipper debate," noted that the "level of vituperation in the attacks against Dorothy Denning . . . [are] at odds with the reasoned . . . things [these postings otherwise] have to say."[5] In addition, Marc Rotenberg from CPSR posted a series of messages that respectfully debated Denning's argument point by point. But in one message where the participant began with a salutation indicating that he may know Denning professionally ("Hi Dorothy"), he later in his otherwise respectful disagreement uses a reference to a young, naive female character in a famous children's story, saying that Denning seems "unnecessarily polly-annish about our government and [Clipper/EES]."[6]

Discussions about Denning and her unpopular point of view continue even today; regular postings about her appear on many of the cryptography newsgroups. In January 1996, for example, one participant on the Cypherpunks list likened her to a "villainess in an Ayn Rand novel."[7] (Note the feminine form of the word *villain*.)

"Smiley Faces" and Women's Language

Overtly misogynist attitudes are only one of the problems concerning gender in the online forums. In addition, many observers are beginning to note that men's and women's conversations via computer are often accompanied by extreme differences in communication style. Many women can speak anecdotally to this difference, and one researcher, linguist Susan Herring, has performed case studies of discourse in cyberspace. She argues that certain features of women's and men's language are apparent in the virtual world. These include women's tendency toward attenuated assertions, apologies, explicit justifications, questions, a personal orientation, and the supporting of others. Men, in contrast, tend to exhibit strong assertions, self-promotion, presuppositions, rhetorical questions, authoritative orientation, challenges to others, and the use of humor or sarcasm (Herring 1993). These features are consistent with what many have argued are the communication differences between women and men in the face-to-face world (Tannen 1990). In cyberspace, however, these features may be heightened by online delivery and what has been called the tendency toward "uninhibited behavior" (Siegel et al. 1986) owing to lack of social cues.

When women did contribute to the online debates over Market-Place and Clipper, their messages illustrate one of Herring's categories, that of attenuated assertions, in their use of the ASCII "smiley face." This symbol is part of a now-familiar feature of discourse in cyberspace: "emoticons."[8] Such emoticons as the key combination :-) are often interjected in a posting to represent physical actions; the previous example, when turned sideways, looks like a smiling face. Emoticons can also indicate vocal inflections; a string of exclamation marks (!!!!!), for example, can be used to indicate an excited pitch. Emoticons have been argued to be replacements for the physical cues normally conveyed in oral discourse (Spitzer 1986, 21; Werry 1993). By using these symbols, participants add to their text a depth not available in a traditionally written memo or letter. In a sense, these symbols make postings look like written conversations. Furthermore, emoticons are frequently used to "attenuate" an assertion, something women often do in spoken conversation by raising their voice at the end of a statement (so the statement sounds like a question, as though the speaker is seeking approval). In the MarketPlace protest, which involved more postings by women than the Clipper protest, it was women who used emoticons in this fashion most frequently, as in the following example:

```
Actually, the idea of taking out a full-page
ad demanding to be removed with a whole lot of
signatures on it and a mail-in coupon to send to
Lotus to demand likewise has a certain charm.
    Time to do a bake sale . . . :-)
```
[9]

The "smiley" after the participant's suggestion regarding a bake
sale (an interesting comment in and of itself with regard to gender)
is inserted to indicate that she is making her suggestion tongue-
in-cheek. Later in this discussion group, after Lotus Corporation
issued a press release announcing it was canceling MarketPlace,
the same woman posted the following message:

> There are a number of things about this press
> release (including the things that AREN'T said) that
> I find pretty intriguing. It's also hilariously
> crocodile-tearish and self-serving, but that's what
> press releases are for, right?:-) [10]

Again, the smiley attenuates the woman's assertion about press releases, emphasizing the question mark at the end of her thought.

The Clipper case presents the same use of emoticons by one of
the few women other than Denning to join the debate. This participant is obviously technically competent about encryption:

> I speculate, from the MykoTronx data sheet on
> the MYK-78, that the algorithm is a classified
> cryptosystem, similar in application to DES but
> cleared by the NSA for classified traffic, that has
> been in use for a number of years. Myktotronx refers
> to it as ''Government Type II encryption,'' which
> matches the designation of one of the types of
> encryption available on STU-III phones, and may be
> the same as a cryptosystem I have heard called
> ''CIPHER2.''
>
> This would make sense, since this is evidently a
> field-proven cryptosystem which can act as a ''pin-
> compatible'' substitute for DES. Combined with a
> tappable key exchange protocol, this would offer
> exactly what is claimed for Clipper: secure
> encryption with access via a key escrow. If this is
> fact the case, it would make me quite confident of
> the encipherment algorithm itself.

She continues in this manner for another paragraph but ends her posting with a classic use of an emoticon:

```
Has anyone else made this sort of connection, or
am I just hallucinating pink elephants here? :).11
```

Her smiley (minus a "nose") is a kind of device found rarely, if at all, among the male participants in the Clipper case, who, instead of attenuating any of their assertions, asserted their opinions strongly.

Dominant Voices, Pornography, and Cyberspace

Some argue that the problem of gender inequity in cyberspace will be solved as more women gain access to the Internet. But, as is often the case in real life (or "IRL," as it's called on the Internet), even in situations when women make up greater numbers of participants, men will often dominate the discussion. This problem has surfaced on numerous occasions on some of the feminist Usenet newsgroups; Kramarae and Taylor (1993) have noted that "in almost any open network, men monopolize the talk," and they indicate that the Usenet newsgroup soc.women is often "overrun" with men (55).[12] This feature further muddies the waters of the cyberlibertarians and the glowing accounts of online communities and their potential.

Finally, it is becoming readily apparent that overtly sexual and sexist material, which can be viewed as pornographic, offensive to women, or even harassing, is readily available in cyberspace. Anyone who has worked in or visited a college computer laboratory has seen the pinups downloaded by male students and used as screensavers or backdrops to their calculus or writing assignments. In addition, documented cases of sexist and misogynist discourse are beginning to surface (Kramarae and Kramer 1995); a lengthy message by four Cornell undergraduates, which originated in 1995, lists the "top 75 reasons why women (bitches) should not have freedom of speech." Concern about the ability to use computers to such ends was expressed during the Lotus MarketPlace protest: many participants worried that the CD-ROM could be used by burglars or rapists to look up single or elderly women. (Although Lotus claimed that users of the product could not identify individuals in this fashion, participants felt it was a real possibility.) Although anger over this possibility was directed at Big Brother Lotus, it appears that all of cyberspace is susceptible to such harassment and sexism.

"Cyberspace, it turns out, isn't much of an Eden after all. It's marred by just as many sexist ruts and gender conflicts as the Real World," reported a major news magazine (Kantrowitz 1994). It is clear from examining both the MarketPlace and Clipper cases that the real-world problems and concerns of gender inequity will not be solved by the technology of computer-mediated communication. In fact, demographics and observations suggest that cyberspace may enhance or magnify already existing gender inequity and sexism. In order for communities in cyberspace to truly fulfill their potential, these issues will have to be addressed. Otherwise, the vision of cyberspace as egalitarian and open will remain valid only in a very limited framework.

8 Big Brother the Corporation and Big Brother the Government

For all its problems, cyberspace continues to offer the potential for rhetorical exchange and social action, as the results of the Lotus MarketPlace and Clipper chip protests reveal. The two cases had decidedly different outcomes: MarketPlace was canceled within just eight months of its announcement and three months of active online debate, while the escrowed encryption standard and Clipper were enacted as a federal standard but continue to be debated and argued against. Although participants in both cases shared an overriding concern with Big Brother, the final outcome of each case shows that "Big Brother the corporation" responded to online action differently from "Big Brother the government."

Lotus Cancels Marketplace

Before canceling its product, Lotus attempted to enter the online debate, but the corporation's attempts were unsuccessful for three reasons. First, Lotus went online too late in the process. By the time the company realized that something was up in cyberspace, the exigence was well defined, a protest community was in place, and postings had traveled across the Internet. Second, Lotus's corporate, top-down style of communication was exactly the opposite of the bottom-up style of the cyberspace protest. Lotus was unable to engage the "organic" structure of the networks and thus could not reach its intended audience. Finally, even when the organization did attempt to post to some conferences, Lotus used

Portions of the section on Lotus MarketPlace in this chapter were previously published as Gurak 1996b and are reprinted with permission from *IEEE Transactions on Professional Communication* 38, no. 1 (March 1995): 2–10. Copyright © 1995 IEEE.

a logical, fact-driven character, using classic "business-ese" and an abstract, impersonal ethos, which was in direct clash with the emotive, informal style of the protest postings and which in fact angered protesters.

Lotus Discovers the Problem

Since the time of the MarketPlace protest, more and more companies have discovered the World Wide Web and other cyberspace forums. Yet the Internet was not as ubiquitous a technology in 1990, and, as a result, Lotus was noticeably absent from the debate in cyberspace. At first, the MarketPlace development team did not make any connection between the Internet and the form letters and phone calls it was receiving about MarketPlace: Households.[1] Although Lotus was a software development company, it did not work with the UNIX operating system, and in 1990 UNIX was the primary system used to support Internet access and, more important, Usenet news. The company was unaware of this significant rhetorical forum for potential debate about its product. Eventually, however, Lotus did learn that the source of the form letters and the cause of the extraordinary number of calls to its toll-free numbers was the Internet-based protest. On January 3, 1991, the company attempted to respond. Yet this response was much too late, given that the protest in cyberspace began on November 14 and the product was canceled on January 23. By January 3, a number of form letters, much discussion, and the email address of Lotus's CEO were readily available on the Internet. The situation had been clearly defined, the community established, and the message, with its truths and its inaccuracies, was well distributed. Only a large-scale, sophisticated rhetorical response by Lotus could have affected the debate at this point. But Lotus's actual response did not have these characteristics.

Corporate Structure in Cyberspace

MarketPlace team members decided to reply to the protest in a way that would provide the most coverage. What newsgroups, they wondered, should they address? How could they "blanket" the network? By the late date of January 3, the debate had spread so widely throughout cyberspace that it was impossible to know where or how to reply. The problem, one former team member indicated, was that they "just couldn't find a coordinated strategy to fight the Internet." The key to this problem is the word *coordinated*. Coordination is just what most corporations want and usually have in their internal communication, but it is exactly what the Internet and this protest were not. The bottom-up nature of the online protest did not conform to the coordinated top-down style of most hierarchically structured organizations.

Lotus based its response on a traditional view of communication, a view incorporating the assumption that it would be possible to reach the public through traditional strategies. Organizations often respond to public controversies in a top-down manner: they issue press releases to the appropriate sources, and this information is dispensed to the public. Even against traditional grassroots protests, which often use call-in and postcard-mailing campaigns, for example, organizations can usually structure a coordinated defense using the traditional mass media and can assume that this approach will reach the public.

Cyberspace, then, must have seemed foreign and uncoordinated to the MarketPlace team. Where was this virtual forum where their product was being so heavily debated, and how could they get there? Once there, how could they be sure they had reached all outlets? Eventually, according to one source, Lotus selected the newsgroup comp.society and posted a note (Former Lotus employee A). Yet because communication on the networks was not organized in a way the corporation could recognize, the MarketPlace team seemed to respond at random, not investigating the Internet and other networks thoroughly and determining what strategy would be most effective. In the uncoordinated Internet structure, they were unable to achieve the coordinated effort they desired. By posting only one message, Lotus was following a traditional top-down corporate communication style. But the protest had spread out across the wide, nonhierarchical Internet, and Lotus's response did not reach any of the protest's most active electronic discussion lists.

The "Hard Facts" Approach of Corporate Rhetoric

Lotus's response was ineffective not only in its delivery but also in its rhetorical appeals. The fact-driven, impersonal, businesslike tone that characterized the posting was in direct clash with the personal and angry ethos of the community of protesters. Furthermore, in creating its arguments in support of MarketPlace, Lotus did not take into account the major concerns of its audience. While mentioning that its database contained nothing more than what other direct-mail databases contain, for example, Lotus failed to recognize that the protesters did not accept the premise that all direct marketing was acceptable.

Lotus's fact driven, logos-based reply is in blatant contrast to the protest postings, and its opening and closing statements are especially striking. Here is the opening paragraph of Lotus's statement:

> In response to recent messages that have appeared
> here about Lotus MarketPlace, we want to provide
> some hard facts that we hope will clear up some of
> the misinformation surrounding our product.[2]

Rather than recognize and address concerns of the protest community, Lotus wants to provide hard facts. Although it is true that some of the protest postings about MarketPlace contained inaccuracies about the product, Lotus followed an ineffective strategy in beginning its reply with a paragraph that appeals to logic, not to the angry and concerned emotions of the protest participants. The entire protest was based on people's personal concerns about MarketPlace. Whether Lotus agreed with these concerns or not, an effective rhetorical strategy would have taken these concerns seriously and responded in kind, speaking to the protest community in their own terms.

Characterizing the protest postings as misinformation was also a tactical error. Again, it is true that some of the postings contained inaccuracies about MarketPlace. But it is also true that many of the postings raised significant questions about MarketPlace and its implications for personal privacy. A thorough review of these postings could have provided Lotus with a sense of how many people were responding to its proposed database. Yet the company's reply ignores this opportunity for dialogue by angering participants through the characterization of their concerns as "misinformation."

The appeals to logic continue throughout the reply, which ends with the following statement:

> We hope that this clarifies any questions or concerns.[3]

This statement refers to the "hard facts" from the opening line of the message. The phrase is impersonal: Lotus seeks to clarify "any questions or concerns" rather than "any of *your* questions or concerns." This statement does not solicit any further input from participants. It does not reflect any understanding of people's fears or anger about MarketPlace. And it does not engage readers with the personal and emotive style used in the protest.

Thus, in both the beginning and the end of the posting (the sections considered most significant in terms of audience appeal), Lotus created a logical, detached, and impersonal ethos. When juxtaposed with the prevailing emotive ethos of the privacy community, this logical ethos did not encourage dialogue between the two sides. Lotus's posting also contained a number of arguments in favor of MarketPlace, which, when combined with the ethos of the posting, heightened anger among participants in the cyberspace protest because the arguments were based on premises the privacy participants did not share.

The following excerpt is from the middle section of Lotus's posting:

Lotus MarketPlace: Households is a CD-ROM database
of names and addresses on U.S. consumers, which
businesses use for direct marketing. It is a small—
but highly visible—part of a multibillion direct
marketing industry that helps businesses deliver
products and services to interested consumers
through compiled lists and databases.

Some people argue that the information collected
in Lotus MarketPlace: Households should not be
available. However, this information is already
readily available, either as a matter of public
record or through thousands of other commercial
lists and database sources. For example, the 1990
Boston Yellow Pages alone lists more than 50 mailing
list brokers.[4]

Later, a similar passage occurs:

Besides limiting the data to what is readily
available as a matter of public record, Census data
profiling, and similar sources . . .[5]

These excerpts contain two implied arguments. The first is that
Lotus is only a small part of the much larger direct-mail marketing
industry. Therefore, because Lotus is only doing what many other
corporations already do, the company's action is not significant or
problematic. Second, Lotus is "small" compared to the "multibillion [dollar]" companies already in this business, although it may
be more visible than its large direct-mail cousins. Continuing in the
same fashion, the next paragraph, and the second excerpt, again
argue that Lotus is only doing what is already being done.

Lotus's argument is deductive, assuming what in rhetorical
theory is called an "enthymeme." This form assumes a premise,
shared by speaker and audience, as the foundation for the rest of
the argument. In the case of the preceding passage, Lotus's argument rests on the premise that many companies provide direct-
mail services and that in doing so they are operating well within

acceptable business standards. Therefore, their argument goes, by also providing direct-mail services, Lotus is doing nothing wrong. Yet Lotus's note does not recognize that most participants did not agree with the premise that direct-mail services or large collections of personal information are acceptable.[6] One participant makes this clear:

> I would point out that the Census is a major
> invasion of privacy in/of/by itself. Data are
> supplied under threat of fine, hardly a symptom of
> a free society. Your claim to being ethical would be
> far stronger were you to drop this source.[7]

That is, this participant explicitly notices that Lotus would more effectively reach its intended audience if it would change the premise of its appeal.

Another ineffective argument in the Lotus posting is its attempt to outline what it called the "privacy controls" that it designed into MarketPlace:

> In developing MarketPlace, Lotus and Equifax
> Marketing Decision Systems have implemented a number
> of controls that go far beyond traditional industry
> practices for consumer privacy protection. Besides
> limiting the data to what is readily available as a
> matter of public record, Census data profiling, and
> similar sources most people can already access, we
> have taken three additional and important steps:
> 1) we are offering the product only to legitimate
> businesses; 2) we are providing consumers with an
> option to have their names removed from the
> database; and 3) we are educating and advising users
> of the proper legal and ethical responsibilities for
> list usage.[8]

Apparently Lotus did not know that this information had already made its way into the privacy community discussion and had been challenged. Many participants, for example, had from the start questioned how Lotus could verify the accuracy of its information and wondered what exactly it defined as a legitimate business. The following response to Lotus's posting illustrates these same concerns:

> [Former Lotus employee A] writes:
>
> > In developing MarketPlace, Lotus and Equifax
> > Marketing Decision Systems
> > have implemented a number of controls that go far
> > beyond traditional
> > industry practices for consumer privacy
> > protection.
>
> Really? Please tell me how I verify that the information about me is correct, and, if wrong, how do I get it corrected? How do you remove someone from the database after you've already sold the CD? How long do you anticipate before someone breaks the encoding method, or otherwise manages to ''steal'' information they did not pay for (or, more importantly, that was supposed to be removed from the database).
>
> > [Also] we are offering the product only to
> > legitimate businesses . . .
>
> And how are you verifying this?[9]

Another participant is similarly concerned with Lotus's encryption scheme:

> I assume you mean that the software provided with the package doesn't provide options for looking up single names or for printing anything other than names and addresses. What if I just don't use your software? What if I write my own software to access the data on the CD-ROM any way I please?
> Perhaps the data is encrypted. Big deal. As another poster has pointed out, it's only a matter

of time before your protection scheme is broken and
made available to the unscrupulous public.[10]

In this posting, such phrases as "big deal" and "unscrupulous
public" are in direct contrast with Lotus's professional ethos. This
participant is thus responding not only to the premise of Lotus's
argument but also to its ethos. In this case and in most of the re-
plies, Lotus clearly added fuel to an already well-burning fire. It
might be said that Lotus was flamed because of its ethos.

Lotus also suggested ways that people can have their names removed from the MarketPlace database and from mailing lists in
general. This topic, too, had already been well debated among the
protest community, and again, one of the participants restated the
general feeling:

> Thank you for providing a means of removing my name
> from your lists. It's kind of a nuisance to have to
> spend my time and postage to do it though. Since
> you're the ones who are going to be making all the
> money from my personal data, it seems as if you
> should have spent *your* time and postage to ask my
> permission to put it there in the first place. I
> know you have no legal obligation to do so—I just
> think it would have been a nice thing to do. Golly,
> you could have used the same envelope to verify that
> your information about me was correct.
>
>   Too expensive, you say? Probably about as
> expensive as all the advertising you're going to buy
> to make that cancellation address known to the
> general public. You are going to take great pains to
> make that option known to the general public, aren't
> you?[11]

One of the criticisms leveled at Lotus in all the online discussions
about MarketPlace was that the company required the public to
be responsible for having their names removed from the product.
Most participants felt that Lotus should be asking the public for

permission to use individual names. But Lotus's reply does not acknowledge this concern, again, no doubt, because the complex structure of the Internet kept Lotus from participating in the debate until this late stage.

When the corporation announced that MarketPlace: Household would be canceled, word spread quickly through the computer conferences. Yet Lotus did not post any notices to the computer conferences. Instead, word of the cancellation came through secondary sources. Participants posted Lotus's press release to the conferences; in one conference, a participant also posted what she claimed was an internal memo of Lotus's. In the press release, Lotus implies that its product was fine but that the public just did not understand:

```
The companies said the decision to cancel the
product came after an assessment of the public
concerns and misunderstanding of the product, and
the substantial, unexpected additional costs
required to fully address consumer privacy issues.
(Lotus Development Corporation 1991)
```

This statement was obviously heard by a conference participant who called Lotus:

```
Perhaps Lotus should rephrase their telephone
announcement as to say the distribution was
cancelled due to the public's UNDERSTANDING of the
product! [12]
```

In the press release, Lotus goes on to explain why it canceled the product, again implying that Lotus's premises were valid:

```
''Unfortunately, Lotus MarketPlace: Households is at
the apex of an emotional firestorm of public concern
about consumer privacy. While we believe that the
actual data content and controls built into the
product preserved consumer privacy, we couldn't
ignore the high level of consumer concern,'' said
```

Jim Manzi, Lotus' president and chief executive
officer. ''After examining all of the issues we have
decided that the cost and complexity of educating
consumers about the issue is beyond the scope of
Lotus as a software provider.'' (Lotus Development
Corporation 1991)

This passage maintains the same "hard facts" approach as Lotus's
earlier posting: we have the facts, the public doesn't, and it would
have been too expensive to consider "educating" consumers about
these facts. This comment continued to aggravate protest participants:

The high-and-mighty tone of that press release
rather annoyed me—it seems to me that they were
saying that most people are just too stupid or
ignorant (about privacy) and that they (Lotus) can't
afford to educate them all. I rather think that if
there is any ignorance or stupidity at all here, it
was in the Lotus and Equifax boardrooms. But
whatever . . .[13]

Press releases, by their very nature, are intended to highlight
an organization's strengths and put what has come to be known as
the "best spin" on a situation; however, it is striking that the corporation continued until the end to ignore the potential of cyberspace. Along with issuing a traditional press release, Lotus could
also have set up an Internet-based chat line or discussion list, or
a Usenet newsgroup in which Lotus representatives participated,
as a way of reaching out to the protesters. Many companies, after
a product failure or public embarrassment, perform these sorts of
outreach efforts. But Lotus maintained its traditional and hierarchical mode of communication.

The Government Implements Clipper

Unlike the MarketPlace case, the Clipper protest did not come to a neat conclusion. The Clipper chip and encryption policy in general continue to be debated, and encryption will likely remain a controversial topic for some time to come. Yet despite the high volume of cyberspace debate and the online petition and other form letters, Clipper was adopted as a federal information-processing standard for voice communications on February 4, 1994, with seemingly little regard for the concerns so clearly expressed by those in the cyberspace privacy communities.

An analysis of the final stages of the Clipper debate reveals three features. First, although there was much online action and discussion, participants were often frustrated by the lack of popular support, which may be related to the technical complexity of Clipper. Second, although the government was aware of the online debate, there was very little government participation on the various Clipper-related forums. Finally, the government enacted the Clipper and EES standard despite its awareness of the online debate and the forty-seven thousand signatures on CPSR's petition.

The Lack of Popular Support

Unlike MarketPlace, Clipper and EES were (are) complicated technologies that do not immediately translate into personal concerns. This complexity led to a much lower level of popular support. Most of the people who signed CPSR's petition did not participate in the online debates and discussions.

The lack of popular support was a source of frustration for many in the privacy community, who expressed concerns similar to those in the following posting from February 1994, just one month before Clipper was implemented as a federal standard (on March 11):

```
I've signed the clipper petition, I've e-mailed
[Senator] Patrick Leahy, but I still don't see any
```

```
POPULAR debate over these attempts to overrun the
Constitution. We need to get creative and get busy.¹⁴
```

Lack of Governmental Participation

The federal government, unlike Lotus Corporation, was well aware of the role of cyberspace in the protest. The *Federal Register* even documented the significance of the cyberspace actions. Yet although the power and potential of cyberspace were clear, government officials ignored or avoided the opportunity to use this space for debate. Most participants in the online debate were those already against Clipper. The few government postings were, like Lotus's, official sounding and impersonal. On occasion the tone of the government's postings was strikingly similar to that of the Lotus message:

```
This new technology will help companies protect
proprietary information, protect the privacy of
personal phone conversations and prevent
unauthorized release of data transmitted
electronically. At the same time this technology
preserves the ability of federal, state and local
law enforcement agencies to intercept lawfully the
phone conversations of criminals.
```

These arguments were easily debated by the privacy activists, who disagreed with the premise that Clipper would protect privacy. They believed Clipper would increase, not preserve, the powers of law enforcement agencies. The government's entire government posting about Clipper reveals a nondialogic, formal message in marked contrast to the kind of heated debate and discussion taking place in the privacy forums. Even where the posting does attempt a dialogic format in the form of questions and answers, its responses are simplistic and do not address the concerns of the privacy community. The question "Who will run the key-escrow data banks?" for example, is answered with the following:

```
The two key-escrow data banks will be run by two
independent entities. At this point, the Department
of Justice and the Administration have yet to
determine which agencies will oversee the key-escrow
data banks.
```

This response was at odds with one of the premises of the privacy advocates, who did not in any way view government agencies as independent. The answer to this question reflects the point of view of the federal government, not those concerned with the privacy implications of Clipper. This reply served only to reinforce the image of government as Big Brother.

Another curious exchange is the following:

```
Q: How do I buy one of these encryption devices?
A: We expect several manufacturers to consider
incorporating the ''Clipper Chip'' into their
devices.
```

The primary concern of most participants was not where they could purchase a Clipper chip but rather how they could keep the product from coming to market in the first place!

The rest of the government posting is similarly out of touch with the concerns of the online privacy community. The government's posting suggests that officials avoided a true opportunity for dialogue in cyberspace and instead relied on conventional communication methods (the formal-sounding press release) and traditional means of seeking public input (meetings and hearings). Thus, each side of the case ended up speaking primarily to themselves. Perhaps government agencies were not ready for the unstructured format of cyberspace dialogue; perhaps they recognized the amount of inaccurate information and heated conversation in cyberspace and did not want to work within this context. Or perhaps it is difficult for any large structured body, be it a corporation or the government, to reshape its communication efforts as quickly as cyberspace has reshaped the discussion forum. Whatever the reason, there was little interaction between government officials and the online privacy advocates.

The Debates Continue over Clipper and EES

Although Clipper and EES were enacted as a standard, they continue to be debated. The newsgroups alt.privacy clipper is still active, and regular postings about Clipper appear on all the privacy newsgroups and mailing lists. The following posting from December 1994 reflects on the aftermath of the CPSR petition and the subsequent implementation of Clipper:

> Why has the government no issued and recognized or
> wide response? Did the CPSR petition mean nothing to
> the government? I'm quite confused as to why no
> action has been taken or seen.[15]

On August 22, 1995, the NIST issued a memorandum requesting input from industry representatives on key escrow issues; this memo circulated around the Internet, often prefaced with the statement "Clipper is back." The new proposal, called "Son of Clipper" or "Clipper II" among privacy advocates, was modified to allow commercial, not governmental, organizations to hold the keys for decryption. Yet this commercial key escrow standard is still controversial, and on November 7, 1995, a group of industry representatives from thirty-seven major technology firms became frustrated with the government's position on encryption and indicated it would create its own encryption policy proposal for the White House to review (Markoff 1995). The November 1995 issue of *Wired* magazine contained an article in its Cyber Rights Now section entitled "Same Old Shit" (Meeks 1995), which characterizes the ongoing frustration over Clipper.

Big Brother in Cyberspace

Corporations now actively use the technologies of the Internet to reach customers, obtain demographics, increase mailing lists, and maintain an advertising presence. Online citizens, especially those in the computer privacy communities, are uncomfortable with this trend toward the commercialization of cyberspace. As more companies assume a place on the Internet, it will be interesting to observe how these organizations function in cyberspace. The Lotus case illustrates that traditional top-down approaches of corporate communication may not work in the virtual forum. In addition, the formal and impersonal corporate ethos is out of place in cyberspace. Lotus's experience with MarketPlace offers a lesson for other companies about the power of community in cyberspace. As Zuboff (1995) has noted, corporations have not paid enough attention to the power of information technologies to change their own traditional structure to more open and participatory ones. Perhaps organizations of the future will see more than marketing possibilities when they look at the communities in cyberspace. Perhaps they will consider using these forums for discussion, focus groups, and feedback.

Government, too, needs to open up to the possibilities for dialogue and participation in cyberspace. In spite of the work of advocacy groups and the development of ad hoc business organizations to express their disagreement with Clipper, government representatives and policy makers seem to have made up their minds to use this method of encryption. Numerous factors point toward a gap between the potential of communication in cyberspace and the government's use of this potential. Many members of Congress still do not have email addresses, and those who do are often slow to respond to the messages they receive. And although private industry has had to come to terms with cyberspace since the time of the MarketPlace controversy, governmental bodies operate under a completely different structure and with completely different motives. What does this suggest for current claims about the potential for online democracy, electronic town halls, and so on?

9 Epilogue: *Privacy, Persuasion, and Communities of the Virtual Future*

The stories of MarketPlace and Clipper leave little doubt that communication in cyberspace has the potential to affect our social, organizational, and political landscapes in ways that are different and perhaps more wide-ranging than any communication technology before. Yet, as current media coverage indicates, people are concerned about what these effects might be. They wonder how to think about the future in light of the onslaught of faster modems, bigger computers, more powerful software, and an ever-increasing number of access points to the Internet. Surveys of Internet usage vary greatly depending on their methodology, but most accounts indicate that the population in cyberspace is growing at a steady pace, both in the United States and worldwide. This trend is evident to those in power: U.S. government discussions about a National Information Infrastructure suggest that computer-mediated communication, widespread as it is today, will become an even more significant backbone of the country's economic and social structure, similar to highways, transportation systems, broadcast airwaves, and telephone lines. Corporations, also aware of the power and potential of communication in cyberspace, are attempting to put a commercial spin on what they see as a new marketplace. Given these competing visions and power bases, it is critical to analyze cases of online discourse now, while the system is still evolving and while policy decisions and legislation are being considered.

The concept of community, particularly how language functions within virtual communities, is one of the most important issues to consider when thinking about cyberspace and the future. Virtual communities extend our ability to connect with people of common interest over distance and time; these virtual bodies thus foreground the intellectual or interest-bound aspect of community, perhaps, it is sometimes suggested, at the expense of physical community. As one futurist has speculated, "Virtual communities are likely to change our experience of the real world—as individuals and communities" (Odgen 1994). One such change may perhaps be the preference of individuals to sit at home and have exciting community interactions over the Internet while never meeting their next-door neighbors. Some are concerned about this tendency and believe that what is needed in today's disjointed society is a return to our obligations and concerns for physical community: neighbors, small businesses, local politics, and so on. Stephen Doheny-Farina (1996), for example, suggests that cyberspace be used for local issues: "The net inspires sweeping proclamations about revolutions, but the constructive power of the net is demonstrated in small ways in local places" (186). He tells us that we should "take part in it [the Net] not to connect to the world but to connect to your city, your town, your neighborhood" (188). Although he is right that sweeping claims are made about the Internet, his suggestions about "staying local" imply that virtual community and physical community still function as separate entities. This thinking ignores the merging of world and neighborhood, physical body and the body in cyberspace, literal next-door neighbor and virtual one—a merging that has already become a part of our social state and consciousness. William Mitchell is not overly deterministic but rather realistic in stating, "We are entering an era of electronically extended bodies living at the intersection points of the physical and the virtual worlds, of occupation and interaction through telepresence as well as through physical presence, of mutant architectural forms that emerge from the telecommunications-induced fragmentation and recombination of traditional architectural types, and of new, soft cities that parallel, complement, and sometimes compete with our existing urban concentrations of brick, concrete, and steel" (1995, 167).

It seems highly unlikely that people will abandon physical community in favor of online connections. Instead, as Mitchell describes it, our interactions will combine the physical and the virtual, the local and the global. In fact, these distinctions may come to have less and less meaning over time. Participants in the Market-Place and Clipper protests were active in their online communities, and many of them, based on their postings, appeared active in their physical communities as well, attending meetings, functioning within corporations and universities, and seeking to raise consciousness about computers and privacy in a context that extended out beyond the computer screen. But it was in cyberspace that these people could connect, talk, make plans, and learn about the topic at hand. People are already moving back and forth from physical to virtual community; the issue is how to shape and use these new structures.

Thus, the problems with virtual community are not about loss of connection to the physical and local. There is something exciting about meeting people from around the world who share your interests or can talk with you about your questions and thoughts. There is something powerful about interacting with people from around the globe, and these possibilities do not necessarily suggest a loss of the physical but a complete change in how we conceive of who we are, where we live, and what we can do. Our primary concern with virtual community should be with how to build on the positive features while dealing with the insularity and extreme specialization that these forums encourage. The MarketPlace and Clipper cases illustrate how closed communities enhance the spread of inaccurate information and how ethos easily becomes dominant in cyberspace. In the political arena, where there is much talk about online democratic action, plans for using cyberspace as a forum for citizen comment and participation should consider this problem. The speed of online delivery and the dominant ethos of certain texts, while powerful in their ability to connect people across vast distance, are not helpful in encouraging open discussions. Who can say, for example, what voices did not enter the debate over Market-Place because they found its ethos too dominant, too one-sided?

This question reflects what should be our fundamental concern with virtual communities. Carolyn Miller (1993), echoing the thoughts of many scholars in rhetoric, composition, and political theory (Clark 1994; Harris 1989; Laclau 1991), characterizes this concern when she asks how we can have communities that are "both pluralist and unified in some important way" (80). In other words, one must ask whether it is possible for communities to allow for disagreement, for dissenting voices, for what Gregory Clark (1994) calls a "rhetoric that directs people to make space for the assertions of others as a part of the process of composing their own" (72). This problem, also articulated by political theorists, is to find a balance between communitarianism, with its emphasis on the needs of a group, and liberalism, with its focus on individual rights (Laclau 1991). The "privileged discourse" that arises in most communities often gives rise to insiders and outsiders (Harris 1989, 15–17), with the insiders quickly establishing an "insider ethos" that is attractive to like-minded individuals but may be unappealing or even silencing to those with dissenting opinions. This ethos is all too common in cyberspace communities; the idea has even been codified in a frequently-asked-questions document (FAQ) called "A Primer on How to Work with the Usenet Community," which gives Internet novices some words of advice on how to become insiders: "The easiest way to learn how to use Usenet is to watch how others use it. Start reading the news and try to figure out what people are doing and why. After a couple of weeks you will start understanding why certain things are done and what things shouldn't be done" (Von Rospach 1994). These instructions imply that people should hang out, assume the dominant ethos, and avoid bringing in any habits that are not generally accepted. We need to work toward systems that encourage the excitement of virtual communities but acknowledge and plan for the difficulties of rhetorical exchange in cyberspace.

We also need to become cautious consumers of online discourse. Politically, much has been made of the notion of cyberdemocracy; many localities and states have projects labeled "electronic democracy" and the like. In considering social actions and petitions in cyberspace, participants need to be aware that the nature of online delivery may encourage a speedy response even though more research on the topic may be in order. "Question authority," a famous saying of the counterculture, should also be a rule in cyberspace:

authority is easily established in the cybercommunity, yet it is not always warranted. In the same regard, students need to learn to be cautious when using Internet material as resources for their papers and projects, and teachers need to learn how to train students to become critical consumers of online information. Courses on civics should now extend to civics in cyberspace: students should learn about such cases as MarketPlace or Clipper and should assess what these actions mean for future citizen participation in a democracy.

The MarketPlace and Clipper cases illustrate that cyberspace communication can take many shapes. We need to ask ourselves how we want our virtual lives structured. The top-down corporate structure is in direct conflict with the shape of most cyberspaces. What would it mean for cyberspace to become more corporate? Should the Internet become a commercial place, where rules and customs of the private sector prevail? Or should virtual communities of the future be modeled after open public forums, where, as with phone lines, content is not regulated? Or can both models co-exist?

The issue of privacy is directly related to these questions. The tools of cyberspace provide the ability to collect and organize massive amounts of information, including personal information. As cyberspace grows and is accessed by more people, the trust once placed in "the Internet community" is being tested on a regular basis. When citizens of the network began a bottom-up discussion about jamming the toll-free phone number for O.J. Simpson's "tell all" video tape, for example, the tape's producer indicated that he had collected the Internet address of every person who wrote such a message and implied that he might sue these people for interfering with business (Deutsch 1996). This attitude is a far cry from the atmosphere of the MarketPlace protest, whose participants were extremely concerned about a CD-ROM but did not imagine that their electronic messages were also being collected for corporate or legal purposes. Encryption, another pressing privacy issue, is also important to the future of online communication, especially if people expect to send such private information as credit card numbers across cyberspace. These concerns need to be dealt with at a high level; as the Commerce Department's 1995 White Paper "Privacy and the NII" indicates, U.S. privacy law is currently ill equipped to handle the changes and possibilities of online interaction.

Issues of identity, too, are highlighted by interactions in cyberspace, where our presence in a community is experienced by others based solely on our thoughts and the ethos we choose to project at that time. One physical individual can have many online personalities, experiencing and exhibiting, in the words of Sherry Turkle, "identity as multiplicity," where "people are able to build a self by cycling through many selves" and where identity is not a single entity but rather a "set of roles that can be mixed and matched" (1995, 180). Yet the technical ability to assume many names and many identities, enjoyed by many in cyberspace, is not in keeping with the desires of those who feel they have a right to know a person's "real" self. In the Clipper case, Mykotronx Corporation might have decided that it wanted to learn exactly who was responsible for anonymously posting its corporate information. Mykotronx did not make such a decision, but the owners of a Caribbean resort recently filed a motion asking America Online to reveal the legal identity of a participant who made what they felt were libelous claims about their services. When considering life in the virtual future, we need to decide how much identity-skewing is to be protected and, in a broader sense, what these multiple personalities mean for communities of the future.

Finally, the concern over access to cyberspace must be a part of any discussion about the future. It demonstrates a certain technocentrism to make claims about community in cyberspace without addressing the fact that many people do not have computers, modems, or even phone lines. It may be that only when cyberspace is as affordable and easy to use as television will it begin to offer broad possibilities for online community. But simply making cyberspace cheaper and easier to use will not remove issues of race, class, gender, physical ability, and so on. Distinctions based on these factors, unlike what is often claimed, are not leveled in the virtual world but, in fact, may be heightened. How to address these issues is a complex question, but we must begin by acknowledging that they exist.

Rhetoric, the art and science of humans communicating, taking action, making reality from our use of symbols, and persuading each other, will look different in the twenty-first century, in part because of the new forums of cyberspace. How this new rhetoric will function depends on how we design, implement, legalize, and use the new tools. The MarketPlace and Clipper cases show that issues of ethos and delivery (at a minimum) will require special attention if we are to have a rhetoric of online discourse that encourages many voices and balances the needs of citizens, government, and corporations. This is a significant time for communication and for community, for public policy and for society in general, and we should use our insights from cyberspace as an opportunity to explore how we might play, work, collaborate, persuade, and take action in communities of the virtual future.

Appendix: *Working and Researching on the Internet*

My adventures with using cybertexts as research data began during the preparation of my Ph.D. dissertation. After gathering the data I wished to use, I turned to a member of my dissertation committee to seek advice about how to cite this material and about whether I needed permission from the authors of the Internet postings. I was told that I probably could answer that question better than she, as I was one of the first to encounter the problem.

I therefore began to learn about intellectual property in cyberspace and various other legal issues I formerly had no background in. As my work in computer-mediated communication has continued, I have corresponded and spoken with numerous lawyers, policy experts, and other researchers. My activities concerning intellectual property issues include co-chairing a national caucus on the subject and working on a university-wide intellectual property committee. I moderate two mailing lists on intellectual property in cyberspace and continue to give considerable thought to the issue of using cybertexts as research data. And now my own graduate students come to me with the same question I asked at the outset of my work. Although the issue has been debated and standards proposed, there is still no definitive policy. We must look to current case law and to standards of research methods until universities, the government, and judges make these issues clearer. Nevertheless, some models exist for using and citing Internet texts.

My approach to using Internet postings in this book balances three forces: respect for privacy, a belief in free access to information, and the reality of copyright in academic publishing. Postings on the Internet, especially those in publicly accessible forums, can be viewed as published material and are increasingly being seen as such by publishers. Yet the intent of an Internet author usually is for his or her material to be seen within the context of the Internet and not in a published research paper or book. As the Internet continues to grow, this expectation will probably vanish, but for this book I aimed to weigh the expectations of authors of Internet postings against the need to use this material for academic purposes. After all, it would be impossible to document these cases without using the postings, and the authors of the postings, being computer experts, were certainly aware that their material would be posted and reposted across cyberspace. And as Edward Cavazos and Gavino Morin (1994) have noted, copyright holds up pretty well in cyberspace, although not all would agree with their claim. What difference does it make, then, if this material, properly credited and in conformance with fair use, is reprinted in a paper document?

I thus followed a procedure that I considered fair. I began by removing the actual email addresses, physical addresses, and references to other persons or corporate affiliations from all the postings. I then changed the name of the author, adding quotes ("Jane Doe") around the changed name in the endnote citation. Other researchers have chosen to make anonymous all material taken from the Internet, and this model is based on the notion that Internet texts are not texts at all but rather written versions of spoken conversations. In some cases, this model is valid: a real-time chat or a MOO or MUD may most resemble conversation, and scholars studying these environments may see themselves as observers of "research subjects"; they would thus be required to follow standard procedures for research involving human subjects (see, for example, Turkle 1995, 321–324). In this book, however, none of the material is from synchronous communication. The postings used here resemble published articles in magazines or newspapers more than spoken conversations, especially in the case of such "digests" as RISKS Digest or Privacy Forum Digest. Therefore, I easily could have made the case that the use of real names in Internet postings was justifiable and legal, and in fact, the part of me that is a scholar concerned with accuracy of primary source material leaned heavily in this direction. In fact, with postings taken

from the WELL, I almost felt compelled to use real names, because the WELL has a policy that authors of postings "own their
own words." Yet WELL founder Howard Rheingold explains that
this statement is not related to issues of citing or authorship; what
it means, he says, is that on the WELL, people are "responsible
for the words they post" and cannot use untraceable pseudonyms
when posting messages (1993b, 74).

Given that the authors of all postings in this book are privacy
advocates who did not expect their postings to go anywhere outside
the Internet, I took the additional step of using pseudonyms. It still
strikes me as odd to have made this choice, as it is highly likely that
more people read these postings on the Internet than ever will read
them in this book. I am sensitive, however, to the current expectations of Internet users, especially privacy advocates, with regard
to their postings. I am also sensitive to the novelty of this issue in
case law. Researchers and university publishers now have little to
base their decisions on, but in our current litigious world and with
so little precedent, it is often wise to err on the side of caution.

During the time I was writing this book, a few World Wide Web
sites began to offer indexes and search tools for locating postings
on Usenet newsgroups. These sites allow users to enter a name,
for example, and find all of the indexed postings to any Usenet
newsgroup by that person. Many online citizens were initially in-
dignant about these tools, yet however you view them, search tools
for Internet material are the next important development in the
technology. All these bits and bytes of information are of no use
unless you can access them (as any librarian will tell you), and it
should come as no surprise that someone (perhaps a researcher,
frustrated by trying to track down Usenet archives) has taken the
time to develop tools to make order out of the disorderly and often
inaccessible Usenet newsgroups. Thus, I would expect that scholars who wish to use publicly accessible Internet texts as their primary source data will feel more and more inclined to use the real
names of the texts' authors, and that these authors will eventually
realize that their postings to the Internet may appear in numerous
other forums. I am sure, given current trends, that universities and

publishers will recognize that Internet postings are for the most part public material, published in a publicly accessible forum, and should therefore be treated as such when it comes to academic criticism and scholarship (see, for example, Stowe 1995, which describes how some university presses are beginning to broaden their view of fair use).

Finally, along with issues of fair use and copyright come concerns about how to cite these Internet postings properly so that scholars, students, and any other interested parties can access the primary data. Such style guides as the *MLA Handbook for Writers of Research Papers* and the *Chicago Manual of Style* have until their most recent editions dealt strictly with traditional printed texts. There are also a number of electronic style sheets available on the World Wide Web. Yet even these sources, which attempt to include information on how to cite electronic texts, do not specifically address the range of sources that one can obtain on the Internet. For this book, I have used a citation method that includes all necessary information about the location of an original text. This appendix contains additional information about how to access specific electronic forums.

The texts themselves are by and large exactly as they were found on the Internet. I have not corrected typographical errors, changed content, or done anything else to alter the original material, with the following exceptions. When texts contained actual email addresses, these were deleted, and the phrase "email address deleted" was inserted in square brackets. When the body of a posting contained a reference to a real person, this person's name was shortened to his or her first initials when appropriate. In addition I removed most authors' real names and replaced them with pseudonyms. These pseudonyms are indicated by the use of square brackets around the name, normally on the "To" line of the note. In the accompanying endnote, the pseudonym is indicated by the use of quotation marks. Finally, electronic discourse of the type analyzed in this book is often replete with typographical errors; however, I did not use "*sic*" within the texts.

Many of the linguistic conventions of communicating on the

Internet are becoming common and are well understood by those who participate in cyberspace regularly; the use of the emoticon to indicate smiles or frowns is one example (see Chapter 7). Other such conventions include the use of the right angle bracket (>) or another character to highlight excerpts of a posting or email message that is being replied to. Also, because typographic characters cannot always be replicated in plain ASCII text, participants often substitute a close approximation, such as a lowercase *o* in place of a bullet. I have replicated these features authentically whenever they occurred in the postings.

Citation Styles for Internet Texts

A standard and formalized system for citing cybertexts does not yet exist. The major style guides include citation methods developed over time for relatively stable material produced in traditional printed forms. Citation styles for television, radio, and electronic databases were later adapted from these basic forms and are now part of most guides. But the rapid proliferation of formats in cyberspace makes it difficult if not impossible for style guides, which are unable to release a new edition every time a new network environment or application appears, to keep up with citations for electronic material.

Elsewhere, I have discussed the complexities of citing electronic texts and made suggestions about sources for students and researchers (Gurak 1996a). In general, the basic formats from an appropriate style guide should be modified with two questions in mind: Is the citation giving appropriate recognition of the original author? and Can another person use the citation to find this same source material?

In this book, Internet texts have been cited with consideration for these two questions and with special thought given to the novelty of online material. Consider the following citation:

> "M———, George." Electronic message to RISKS Digest 10.61. November 16, 1990. Posted November 14, 1990, 09:19:28 EDT.

In this case, a message by "George M." (a pseudonym) was published in volume 10, issue 61, of RISKS Digest. But "George M." could easily have sent more than one message to this same issue of the digest. Therefore, in order to distinguish the cited message from any other, the original date and time of his posting is added. Some researchers have suggested that the subject line of the message should be used as the distinguishing field, but often people post many messages on the same date with the same subject line. Another reason for including the date posted and the date of publication is to document the time between the sending of the original posting and the publication of the online magazine by the digest moderator.

In another example, slightly different information is used:

"K——, Tom." Electronic message to Whole Earth 'Lectronic Link computer conference, Electronic Frontier Foundation conference, topic 71 (Lotus MarketPlace). November 14, 1990. Message no. 0. 1:33 PST.

The WELL's system provides individual message numbers (in this case 0, the first message), which can be used to identify a specific message. The date posted and the date of appearance on the forum are the same, because this particular forum was not moderated (that is, no one reviewed the messages before they were posted). Finally, the time of posting is added for accuracy's sake.

Other variations of this method are used in the citations in this book.

Newsgroups and Mailing Lists Used in This Book

Some of the primary sources used in this book are available only on Usenet, others are available only on a listserv, still others are available only on Web pages or at ftp or gopher sites, and some are available in numerous forms (table A.1). For more information on using listserv, Usenet news, the World Wide Web, or other Internet tools, consult a good reference book on the Internet (available in any local bookstore's computer section).

Table A.1. Newsgroups and Mailing Lists Used in This Book

Forum	Brief Description [a]	Discussion List	Usenet Newsgroup	WWW and Other Sites
Cypherpunks	Informal group that develops technological solutions to protect privacy. The Cypherpunks write cryptography and discuss political and technical issues	Send message consisting of the words "subscribe cypherpunks" (quotes not included) to: majordomo@toad.com	nntp://nntp.hks.net/ hks.lists.cypherpunks	WWW: http://www.hks.net/cpunks/ index.html FTP: ftp.csua.berkeley.edu/pub/ cypherpunks/Home.html
Privacy Forum Digest	Moderated digest for discussion and analysis of issues relating to the general topic of privacy in the "information age" of the 1990s and beyond. Supported in part by ACM Committee on Computers and Public Policy, and the Data Services Division of MCI Communications Corporation	Send message consisting of the word "help" (quotes not included) in the body of a message to: privacy-request@vortex.com	Not available as Usenet newsgroup	WWW: http://www.vortex.com FTP: ftp.vortex.com directory/privacy Gopher: vortex.com

Forum	Brief Description[a]	Discussion List	Usenet Newsgroup	WWW and Other Sites
Privacy/Clipper newsgroup	Unmoderated Usenet newsgroup on issues related to Clipper and privacy	Not available as list	alt.privacy.clipper	None available
Computer Privacy Digest	Moderated forum for discussion on the effect of technology on privacy	Send message consisting of the word "subscribe" (quotes not included) to: com-privacy-request@uwm.edu	comp.society.privacy	FTP: ftp.cs.uwm.edu/pub/comp-privacy Gopher: cs.uwm.edu
Cryptography newsgroup	Unmoderated Usenet newsgroup on issues related to cryptography and politics	Not available as list	talk.politics.crypto	None available
RISKS Digest	Moderated forum on risks to the public in computers and related systems. Supported by the ACM Committee on Computers and the Public	Preferred method of access is via Usenet, but for more information about the listserv format, send a message to risks-request@csl.sri.com	comp.risks	FTP: ftp unix.sri.com directory /risks

Organization	Description	Online newsletter	Usenet	Web/FTP/Gopher
Electronic Privacy Information Center (EPIC)	An organization established in 1994 to focus public attention on emerging privacy issues relating to the National Information Infrastructure	EPIC online newsletter: send email to info@epic.org	Not available as Usenet newsgroup	WWW: http://www.epic.org/
Electronic Freedom Foundation (EFF)	An organization founded in 1990 to maintain and enhance intellectual freedom, privacy, and other values of civil liberties and democracy in networked communications	EFFector online newsletter: send email to info@eff.org	comp.org.eff.talk	WWW: http://www.eff.org/ FTP: ftp.eff.org Gopher: eff.org
Computer Professionals for Social Responsibility (CPSR)	A national membership organization of people concerned about the impact of technology on society. It has 24 local chapters across the U.S. and several international affiliates	CPSR online newsletter: send email to cpsr-info@cpsr.org	comp.org.cpsr.announce	WWW: http://cpsr.org/cpsr FTP: ftp.cpsr.org Gopher: cpsr.org

Forum	Brief Description[a]	Discussion List	Usenet Newsgroup	WWW and Other Sites
The Whole Earth 'Lectronic Link (WELL)	A computer network based in Sausalito, California	Telnet to well.sf.ca.us to sign up	Not available as Usenet newsgroup	None available
U.S. government information	Includes Library of Congress records, information about bills, and other information	Not available as list	Not available as Usenet newsgroup	WWW: http://www.loc.gov/ Gopher: marvel.loc.gov

Note: The information in this table is extremely subject to change.

[a]Descriptions are taken from online sources provided by each group.

NOTES

1. *Cyberspace* has become a common word used to designate the virtual places and spaces on the Internet. The term was coined by William Gibson (1991) in his science fiction novel *Neuromancer.*

2. Much of this work falls into the category of a social-psychological approach to the study of CMC.

3. There is a large body of work on the notion of discourse community, including Bruffee 1986; Harris 1989; Lyon 1992; Porter 1992; Reynolds 1993; and Swales 1990.

4. "D——, David." Electronic message to Whole Earth 'Lectronic Link computer conference, Electronic Frontier Foundation conference, topic 71 (Lotus MarketPlace). March 24, 1991. Message no. 278. 09:16 PST.

5. Turkle (1995) provides a thorough and extremely interesting description and analysis of MUDs and MOOs, with regard not only to their sense of place and space but also to their impact on human psychology and sense of identity.

6. Swales's (1990) six characteristics of discourse community also apply to this discussion. These characteristics are: (1) a broadly agreed upon set of common public goals, (2) mechanisms of intercommunication, (3) participatory mechanisms, (4) possession of one or more genres, (5) a specific lexis of communication, and (6) changing memberships (24–27).

7. "J——, Brad." Electronic message to comp.os.msdos.misc Usenet newsgroup. June 21, 1993. 02:10:36 GMT.

8. Greek and Roman rhetors, specifically those associated with Aristotle and Quintilian or Cicero, had distinctly different ideas about ethos, however. Whereas Aristotle's rhetoric spoke primarily of finding the available means and using them, Romans such as Quintilian or Cicero placed far greater emphasis on the rhetor as someone who embodied civic good (Johnson 1984). Yet my point here is that the general notion of ethos as character has been a strong part of the entire classical tradition and has been carried down into contemporary rhetorical theory.

147

9. Burke (1969) invokes ethos when he suggests that speakers establish credibility and character through common values with the audience, seen in his example of the "politician who, addressing an audience of farmers, says 'I was a farm boy myself' " (xiv). Although Burke's notion of identification as cooperation is ideologically much different from Aristotle's theory of persuasion, the belief in the importance of a rhetor's character and of values a rhetor shares with his or her audience is common to both the classical and contemporary traditions.

10. Some debate has concerned how to interpret ethos in this regard: as the character of the speaker himself or herself, or as the character that is conveyed through the speech. Some translations of Aristotle, for example, have been interpreted to mean that ethos involved not the character of the speaker but rather the way the speech was delivered (Baumlin 1994, xv). Kennedy's translation, however, indicates that for Aristotle ethos "is regarded as an attribute of a person, not a speech" (Aristotle, p. 37).

11. In classical rhetoric, delivery was one of five canons, or parts, of the rhetorical system. Ethos, for example, was part of the first canon of invention. The next two canons, arrangement and style, involved how a speech was organized and in what stylistic manner it was constructed. The final two canons, memory and delivery, were especially important to ancient rhetors, for whom public speaking involved a good memory and an ability to deliver before a live audience.

12. Both the fourth canon of memory and the fifth canon of delivery have traditionally received little theoretical treatment in English studies; in regard to writing, Connors (1993) notes that the "status of the last two [rhetorical canons], memory and delivery, has always been problematic" (65). Speech communication has provided a bit more theory on delivery, dating back to elocutionary training by such teachers as Thomas Sheridan (1719–1788) and Gilbert Austin (1753–1837) and to the later use of the Delsarte method in the late 1800s and early 1900s to teach theater and oratory. A similar focus is found currently in studies of nonverbal communication and human gesture. Yet in general, it is fair to say that the fifth canon, when compared to invention or style, has suffered from a rather impoverished rhetorical history.

13. See, for example, Hiltz and Turoff 1993; Lea et al. 1992; Rice and Love 1987; and Sproull and Kiesler 1986, 1993.

Chapter 2: The Case of Lotus MarketPlace

1. Unless otherwise noted, the specifications and quotations about Market-Place used in this chapter are based on a series of press releases issued by Lotus during the announcement of the product and its cancellation.

2. Neither of these options will guarantee accuracy or removal from all databases; the vast web of private direct-mail databases in the United States is far too complex and unregulated to ensure that a name will be permanently removed. Nevertheless, making changes on a database is possible, whereas making changes on CD-ROM is virtually impossible.

3. Unless otherwise noted, information in this section is based on a telephone interview with one of the original members of the MarketPlace development team (former Lotus employee A 1993).

4. The names of former Lotus employees have been changed to "former Lotus employee A" and "former Lotus employee B." Both of these former employees were part of the MarketPlace development team.

5. "H——, Steven L." Electronic message to tcp-ip Usenet newsgroup. January 3, 1990. 12:54:45 PST.

6. When messages are posted to computer conferences or sent as email, they are prefaced with identifier material known as the header, which is similar to the top portion of a memo but with more information. The header usually contains the name and email address of the sender, the sender's affiliation, the subject of the message, the place where the message originated, the date and time when the message was sent, and a message identifier number. As a note is forwarded, new headers are appended at the beginning of the message. The copy that I obtained of the note providing Manzi's address has four headers before the original header.

7. This information was verified by an interview with former Lotus employee B (1993).

8. This number was widely cited in the media (Fisher 1991a) and was confirmed by an interview with former Lotus employee B (1993).

9. "F——, Nora." Electronic message to Whole Earth 'Lectronic Link computer conference, Electronic Frontier Foundation conference, topic 71 (Lotus MarketPlace). January 28, 1991. Message no. 267. 10:51 PST.

10. "K——, Jim." Electronic message to Telecom Digest 11.63. January 24, 1991. 13:28:58 PST.

11. Townson, Patrick A. (digest moderator). Electronic message to Telecom Digest. January 25, 1991.

Chapter 3: The Case of the Clipper Chip

1. Unless otherwise noted, information and quotations in this chapter were obtained from a *New York Times* article by science and technology reporter John Markoff (1993), who provided excellent coverage of the Clipper chip controversy.

2. This section covers only the basics. For a more detailed explanation of the encryption process, see, for example, Denning 1983; Hoffman 1985; Kahn 1972; and Schneier 1994.

3. For the purposes of this book, I will discuss the "protest over Clipper" or the "debates about Clipper," but in fact, what was often at issue was not simply the chip itself but the more general EES. Yet the debate on the Internet came to be known as the Clipper chip controversy.

4. The debate continued past the one-year mark, but it was during the period April 1993–March 1994 that most significant events took place.

5. Reports vary on the actual number of signatures. The Electronic Privacy Information Center (EPIC), a CPSR-sponsored organization, reported forty-seven thousand signatures from more than three thousand Internet sites, while the major print media reported anywhere from forty-five thousand to fifty thousand signatures. Depending on how many versions of the petition were circulating and how many versions were ultimately delivered to the White House, each of these figures could in a sense be correct. Even after a single version was delivered, other versions might still have been circulating and gathering signatures. The variation in the signature counts points out a significant difference between traditional paper texts and interactive electronic texts; the fixed nature of the the first is replaced by a dynamic quality in the second.

6. Banisar, Dave. Electronic message to PACS-L electronic discussion list. February 2, 1994. 14:11:47 CST.

7. "F——, Doug." Electronic message to Computer Privacy Digest 2.34. April 19, 1993. Posted April 17, 1993, 19:31:05 GMT.

8. Anonymous. Information on Mykotronx received from anonymous source 5.93. May 1993. Available via anonymous ftp from ftp.cpsr.org/cpsr/privacy/crypto/clipper/mykotronics__info.txt.

Chapter 4: Exigence in Cyberspace

1. This concept of rhetorical situation was later critiqued as being too foundationalist and ignoring human agency and social construction; as one commentator put it, "No situation can have a nature independent of the perception of its interpreter or independent of the rhetoric with which he chooses to characterize it" (Vatz 1973, 154). Yet the blending of Bitzer's original observation with the notion of human and social agency has added a significant element to rhetorical theory. Rhetoric is more than speaker and audience; exigence, as constructed and understood by speaker and audience, defines the situation and provides a context in which all participants function. I thus suggest that the concept of rhetorical situation is perhaps more complicated than both Bitzer and his critics believed. The Lotus and Clipper cases provide support for the notion that exigencies are not just "out there" as a kind of Platonic form but are instead socially constructed based on the context and the interpretations of speaker and audience.

2. See, for example, Westin and Baker 1972, one of the earliest texts.

3. *Olmstead v. United States*, 277 U.S. 438, 478 (1928) (Brandeis, J., dissenting).

4. Not only was computer privacy an issue, but broader concerns about personal privacy (regarding urine and blood sampling, AIDS testing, and such technologies as caller ID) were also prevalent at this time.

5. From an informational brochure published by CPSR.

6. "M———, George." Electronic message to RISKS Digest 10.61. November 16, 1990. Posted November 14, 1990, 09:19:28 EDT.

7. "K———, Tom." Electronic message to Whole Earth 'Lectronic Link computer conference, Electronic Frontier Foundation conference, topic 71 (Lotus MarketPlace). November 14, 1990. Message no. 0. 1:33 PST.

8. The entire process of forwarding a message takes only a minute or two and requires less than ten keystrokes. This process is thus one illustration of Kaufer and Carley's (1994) principles of distance communication in relation to delivery. First, the principle of multiplicity, which they define as the "number of communication partners that can be communicated with at the same time," is illustrated by the many people who read the early postings. Second, availability of these messages to anyone at any time shows "asynchronicity": the freeing of network participants "from having

to work at the same time," thus overcoming the distances of both time and space (34).

9. "P——, Geoff." Electronic message to RISKS Digest 10.61. November 16, 1990. Posted November 14, 1990, 09:53:47 PST.

10. "A——, Stan Jacob." Electronic message to RISKS Digest 10.61. November 16, 1990. Posted November 15, 1990, 09:47:13.

11. Some, but not all, computer conferences have moderators who play the role of editor and who often screen out messages deemed inappropriate for the conference. Moderators can help weed out the high volume of junk mail that is often posted to unmoderated conferences, yet some people feel that moderators also act as censors.

12. "S——, Earl." Electronic message to Computer Privacy Digest 2.37. April 27, 1993. Posted April 17, 1993, 14:04:30.

13. "U——, Harry." Electronic message to Computer Privacy Digest 2.38. April 27, 1993. Posted April 25, 1993, 18:17:58.

14. "N——, R." Electronic message to RISKS Digest 14.51. April 21, 1993. Posted April 20, 1993, 10:45 GMT.

15. "M——, George." Electronic message to Privacy Forum Digest 3.5. February 27, 1994. Posted on February 21, 1994, 08:20:22 EDT.

16. One of the ways the Greek *ethos* can be translated is "habitual gathering place" (Halloran 1982; Reynolds 1993), which makes perfect sense for such online social spaces as newsgroups, where the habits of how to communicate are learned by inhabiting the space and paying attention to the ethos of the other speakers.

17. In some instances, speakers in the privacy conferences did not agree with the majority opinion about Lotus MarketPlace. Yet everyone in the conferences appears to have been knowledgeable about privacy issues, and the overwhelming majority of the speakers were against the Lotus product.

18. "K——, Tom." Electronic message to Whole Earth 'Lectronic Link computer conference, Electronic Frontier Foundation conference, topic 71 (Lotus MarketPlace). December 20, 1990. Message no. 153–154. 19:22 PST.

19. "P——, Brice." Electronic message to Privacy Forum Digest 2.12. April 17, 1993. Posted April 16, 1993, 16:59:16.

20. "R——, B. Roger." Electronic message to Privacy Forum Digest 2.13. April 22, 1993. Posted April 18, 1993, 09:44:41. "IMHO" is a common online acronym for "in my humble opinion."

21. "L——, Adam S." Electronic message to Privacy Forum Digest 2.15. April 30, 1993. Posted April 24, 1993, 13:03:46.

22. "N——, Todd." Electronic message to Computer Privacy Digest 2.38. April 30, 1993. Posted April 28, 1993, 19:16:01.

23. "G——, Rob." Electronic message to Privacy Forum Digest 2.15. April 30, 1993. Posted April 28, 1993, 11:19:44.

24. "F——, Doug." Electronic message to Computer Privacy Digest 2.34. April 19, 1993. Posted April 17, 1993, 19:31:05 GMT.

Chapter 5: Structures of Online Communication

1. Researchers studying the novel dynamics of online communication have since the beginning been interested in the notion of leadership and dominance in these electronic forums. Hiltz and Turoff (1993), in their now-classic work on computer conferencing, conclude that "unless a moderator takes hold and sets an agenda and keeps the group working toward its goal, nothing much will occur within a [computerized] conference" (124), but others have argued that hierarchy and centralized authority in cyberspace are replaced by more bottom-up structures (Sproull and Kiesler 1993). It is clear from an examination of the Lotus and Clipper cases that it may not be possible to generalize about structure and authority in online forums, because, as in all human communication situations, context and existing social and organizational forces play significant roles in power relations online, as noted by Spears and Lea (1994), among others.

2. "K——, Tom." Electronic message to Whole Earth 'Lectronic Link computer conference, Electronic Frontier Foundation conference, topic 71 (Lotus MarketPlace). November 14, 1990. Message no. 0. 1:33 PST.

3. "B——, Frank." Electronic message to RISKS Digest 10.62. November 19, 1990. Posted November 16, 1990, 11:38:37 PST.

4. Kapor, Mitch. Electronic message to Whole Earth 'Lectronic Link computer conference, Electronic Frontier Foundation conference, topic 71 (Lotus MarketPlace). November 19, 1990. Message no. 20. 20:07 PST. Kapor is one of the founders of Lotus Corporation. His presence on this discussion group thus adds credibility to the forum.

5. "F——, Nora." Electronic message to Whole Earth 'Lectronic Link computer conference, Electronic Frontier Foundation conference, topic 71 (Lotus MarketPlace). November 21, 1990. Message no. 26. 08:30 PST.

6. "H——, William." Electronic message to Whole Earth 'Lectronic Link computer conference, Electronic Frontier Foundation conference, topic 71 (Lotus MarketPlace). November 21, 1990. Message no. 27. 09:43 PST.

7. "F——, Nora." Electronic message to Whole Earth 'Lectronic Link computer conference, Electronic Frontier Foundation conference, topic 71 (Lotus MarketPlace). November 21, 1990. Message no. 28. 09:52 PST.

8. "D——, Dave." Electronic message to Whole Earth 'Lectronic Link computer conference, Electronic Frontier Foundation conference, topic 71 (Lotus MarketPlace). November 21, 1990. Message no. 36. 18:33 PST.

9. Rotenberg, Marc. Electronic message to Whole Earth 'Lectronic Link computer conference, Electronic Frontier Foundation conference, topic 71 (Lotus MarketPlace). December 4, 1990. Message no. 82. 19:02 PST.

10. Seiler, Larry. Electronic letter distributed to many sites on the Internet. Excerpted from Seiler's original posting and used here with permission. December 2, 1990.

11. I have documented numerous "echoes" of Seiler's letter in various edited forms, including December 20 on the WELL and December 30 on both Telecom Digest and Telecom Privacy Digest.

12. "K——, Tom." Electronic message to Whole Earth 'Lectronic Link computer conference, Electronic Frontier Foundation conference, topic 71 (Lotus MarketPlace). December 20, 1990. Message no. 153–154. 19:22 PST.

13. "D——, Robert C. Electronic message to Telecom Privacy Digest 2.11. January 23, 1991. 7:32:32 PST.

14. Rears, Dennis G. (digest moderator). Electronic message to Computer Privacy Digest 2.35. April 24, 1993. 15:12:56 EDT.

15. "F——, Doug." Electronic message to Computer Privacy Digest 2.34. April 19, 1993. Posted April 17, 1993, 19:31:05 GMT.

16. "Z——, Harold." Electronic message to alt.security.pgp Usenet newsgroup. April 28, 1993. 21:00:45 GMT.

17. "D——, Greg." Electronic message to PACS-L electronic discussion list. 3 Feb. 1993 14:46:24 CST.

18. "L——, Paul." Electronic message to Whole Earth 'Lectronic Link computer conference, Electronic Frontier Foundation conference, topic 71 (Lotus MarketPlace). November 19, 1990. Message no. 23. 22:54 PST.

19. For reasons unrelated to the MarketPlace incident, on October 11, 1995, Manzi resigned from IBM, where he had become a senior vice president after that company bought out Lotus Development Corporation in June 1995.

20. "H——, Steven L." Electronic message to tcp-ip computer conference. January 3, 1990. 12:54:45 PST.

21. Banisar, Dave. Electronic message to PACS-L electronic discussion list. February 2, 1994. 14:11:47 CST.

22. "P——, Robert." Electronic message to Computer Privacy Digest 2.48. June 3, 1993. Posted June 2, 1993, 20:59:24 EDT.

23. "P——, Robert." Electronic message to Computer Privacy Digest 2.48. June 3, 1993. Posted June 2, 1993, 20:59:24 EDT.

24. I have removed Seiler's home address and the rest of the last names and addresses he listed in the letter.

25. Seiler, Larry. Electronic letter distributed to many sites on the Internet. Excerpted from Seiler's original posting and used here with permission. December 2, 1990.

26. "T——, Mike." Electronic message to Whole Earth 'Lectronic Link computer conference, Electronic Frontier Foundation conference, topic 71 (Lotus MarketPlace). November 21, 1990. Message no. 25. 06:33 PST.

27. "S——, Bart." Electronic message to Whole Earth 'Lectronic Link computer conference, Electronic Frontier Foundation conference, topic 71 (Lotus MarketPlace). December 22, 1990. Message no. 71. 18:07 PST.

28. Seiler, Larry. Electronic letter distributed to many sites on the Internet. Excerpted from Seiler's original posting and used here with permission. December 2, 1990.

29. Anonymous. Information on Mykotronx received from anonymous source 5.93. Available via anonymous ftp from ftp.cpsr.org/cpsr/privacy/crypto/clipper/mykotronics__info.txt.

Chapter 6: Ethos, Flaming, and Inaccuracy

1. The model also incorporates the assumption that all people, regardless of gender, class, or age, participate equally in cyberspace, a notion that is strongly challenged in the next chapter.

2. Seiler, Larry. Electronic letter distributed to many sites on the Internet. Excerpted from Seiler's original posting and used here with permission. December 2, 1990.

3. In one study, Siegel et al. (1986), defining *uninhibited* as instances of "swearing, insults, and name-calling," noted that participants on computer forums were "more uninhibited than were [people] communicating face to face" (174). Others have also noted that the "lack of nonverbal cues about physical appearance, authority, status, and turn-taking allows users to participate . . . more equally *and with more extreme affect* on CMC systems than in many face-to-face interactions" (emphasis added; Rice and Love 1987, 89). Much of the research on flaming from the perspective of the social sciences has focused on answering the question of *why* this phenomenon occurs on computer networks. Lea et al. (1992) classify the results of this research into two general areas: reduced social cues and the values and norms of the computing subculture (92–94). Feminist researchers have taken a different approach, suggesting that flaming may be caused by a masculine style of communicating (Herring 1993). This suggestion is definitely open for more research.

4. Exact author unclear; excerpted into the following posting: "D——, Robert C." Electronic message to Telecom Privacy Digest 2.11. January 23, 1991. 7:32:32 PST.

5. Seiler, Larry. Electronic letter distributed to many sites on the Internet. Excerpted from Seiler's original posting and used here with permission. December 2, 1990.

6. Exact author unclear; excerpted into the following posting: "D——, Robert C." Electronic message to Telecom Privacy Digest 2.11. January 23, 1991. 7:32:32 PST. Because of the nature of online writing and delivery, it is difficult to know how to give credit properly for certain online postings such as the one cited here. The excerpt of this posting was copied by two people before being pasted into the final note. I have given credit to the person who posted the final note, although this person is not the author of the passage cited.

7. "J——, Don." Electronic message to Telecom Privacy Digest 2.15. February 1, 1991. 12:03:00 EDT.

8. Townson, Patrick A. (digest moderator). Electronic message to Telecom Digest. December 30, 1990.

9. "T——, Matt." Electronic message to Telecom Privacy Digest 1.42. December 31, 1990. Posted December 30, 1990, 14:59:48 PST.

10. "R——, Seth J." Electronic message to Telecom Privacy Digest 2.1. January 2, 1991. Posted December 31, 1990. 08:10:06.

11. "N——, Matt." Electronic message to Whole Earth 'Lectronic Link computer conference, Electronic Frontier Foundation conference, topic 71 (Lotus MarketPlace). November 14, 1990. Message no. 4. 16:03 PST.

12. Weinstein, Lauren (digest moderator). Electronic message to Privacy Forum Digest 3.4. February 20, 1994. 12:57 PST.

13. Weinstein, Lauren (digest moderator.) Electronic message to Privacy Forum Digest 3.5. February 27, 1994. Posted February 22, 1994, 20:22 PST.

14. Rotenberg, Marc. Electronic message to Privacy Forum Digest 3.5. February 27, 1994.

15. "M——, George." Electronic message to Privacy Forum Digest 3.5. February 27, 1994. Posted February 21, 1994, 08:20:22 EDT.

16. "G——, Satish." Electronic message to Privacy Forum Digest 3.5. February 27, 1994. Posted February 24, 1994, 09:36:56.

Chapter 7: Gender in Cyberspace

1. It is impossible to know for sure the gender of a participant, because it is easy to change one's identity on the Internet (see Turkle 1995 for more on "gender bending" in cyberspace). Linguist Susan Herring (1993) uses surveys to determine the actual gender of the author of an online posting. For this chapter, I have informally communicated with some but not all participants in the MarketPlace and Clipper cases. It is obvious from the debates themselves that many participants were very proud of their postings and affiliations. I therefore believe that most participants were using their real names, and my claim that most participants were men is based on the names used in the postings. Obviously, some of the postings claimed to be by men could in fact be by women, although anecdotal observations

indicate that it is usually men who pose as women in cyberspace, not the other way around (Turkle 1995, 223).

2. Unfortunately, most of the talk about Denning took place on the newsgroup alt.privacy.clipper, which is not archived. This section of the book is therefore much shorter than it would otherwise be. According to postings on other newsgroups, however, alt.privacy.clipper contained some intense debates about Denning. I have reconstructed some material of these debates, based on what I could locate.

3. "L——, Kevin J." Electronic message to RISKS Digest 14.64. May 19, 1993. 16:32:46 EDT.

4. "L——, Kevin J." Electronic message to RISKS Digest 14.64. May 19, 1993. 16:32:46 EDT.

5. "M——, George." Electronic message to Privacy Forum Digest 3.5. February 27, 1994. Posted February 21, 1994, 08:20:22 EDT.

6. "D——, Dean." Electronic message to Privacy Forum Digest 3.5. February 27, 1994. Posted by Dave Banisar (with permission) on February 25, 1994, 22:43:48 EST.

7. "N——, Bert." Electronic message to cypherpunks@toad.com. Reposted January 27, 1996, 16:49:40.

8. Emoticons are referred to in numerous introductory Internet books, and a number of Web sites contain information about various emoticons that can be made with ASCII characters.

9. "F——, Nora." Electronic message to Whole Earth 'Lectronic Link computer conference, Electronic Frontier Foundation conference, topic 71 (Lotus MarketPlace). November 21, 1990. Message no. 28. 09:52 PST.

10. "F——, Nora." Electronic message to Whole Earth 'Lectronic Link computer conference, Electronic Frontier Foundation conference, topic 71 (Lotus MarketPlace). January 23, 1991. Message no. 244. 13:43 PST.

11. "H——, Tamara." Electronic message to alt.security.pgp Usenet newsgroup. April 29, 1993. 01:08:02.

12. Herring's study (1993) also suggests this phenomenon.

Chapter 8: The Corporation and the Government

1. Material in this section is based primarily on interviews with former MarketPlace team members (former Lotus employees A and B).

2. Former Lotus employee A writing for the company. Electronic message to comp.society Usenet newsgroup. January 3, 1991. 18:14:15 GMT.

3. Former Lotus employee A writing for the company. Electronic message to comp.society Usenet newsgroup. January 3, 1991. 18:14:15 GMT.

4. Former Lotus employee A writing for the company. Electronic message to comp.society Usenet newsgroup. January 3, 1991. 18:14:15 GMT.

5. Former Lotus employee A writing for the company. Electronic message to comp.society Usenet newsgroup. January 3, 1991. 18:14:15 GMT.

6. Lotus's argument does not address the most basic understanding of how to engage an audience. In rhetorical theory, the enthymeme is where speakers identify a common experience with their audience and use that experience as the shared premise in their deductive argument (Aristotle, 1396a). This notion of enthymeme has been suggested to invite dialogue because it asks audiences to participate in the formation of the major premise (Bitzer 1959; Raymond 1984; Walker 1994). Aristotle and contemporary theorists, then, agree that the major premise implied in an enthymeme should appeal to its intended audience.

7. "C——, Grant." Electronic message to comp.society Usenet newsgroup. January 4, 1991. 01:09:32 GMT.

8. Former Lotus employee A writing for the company. Electronic message to comp.society Usenet newsgroup. January 3, 1991. 18:14:15 GMT.

9. "M——, Timothy Evan." Electronic message to comp.society Usenet newsgroup. January 3, 1991. 08:18:43 GMT.

10. "S——, Ronald." Electronic message to comp.society Usenet newsgroup. January 4, 1990. 01:07:48 GMT.

11. "S——, Ronald." Electronic message to comp.society Usenet newsgroup. January 4, 1990. 01:07:48 GMT.

12. "G——, Steven J." Electronic message to Telecom Privacy Digest 2.14. February 1, 1991. Posted January 30, 1991. 18:04 EST.

13. "D———, Dave." Electronic message to Whole Earth 'Lectronic Link computer conference, Electronic Frontier Foundation conference, topic 71 (Lotus MarketPlace). January 24, 1991. Message no. 260. 19:45 PST.

14. "G———, Paul N." Electronic message to Computer Privacy Digest 4.36. March 1, 1994. Posted February 27, 1994, 19:37:07 GMT.

15. "A———, Wyatt." Electronic message to alt.privacy.clipper Usenet newsgroup. December 30, 1994. 01:18:52 GMT.

GLOSSARY

Anonymous ftp: A procedure by which users sign on to a remote computer with the login name "anonymous" and then transfer files from this remote site to their local computer. *See also* FTP.

Archive: A file or directory used to hold other files, such as back files of Usenet newsgroups. Also, the act of placing files into an archive or of compressing files so they will fit in an archive.

Asynchronous communication: Communication over computers in which data being sent and data being received are transferred without a predictable time relationship. Asynchronous communications therefore do not take place in real time. *See also* Synchronous communication.

Bulletin board: A discrete system, most often based on one computer, into which users can dial and post notices, read information, and correspond. Bulletin boards generally are dedicated to a specific topic.

Chat: *See* Real-time chat.

CMC: *See* Computer-mediated communication.

Comp.society: A Usenet newsgroup containing postings about general issues related to computers and society.

Computer-mediated communication (CMC): Communication between humans using computers and related software. CMC can include email; real-time chats (synchronous communication); bulletin boards, lists, and newsgroups (asynchronous communication); conferencing systems; and local networks (such as the WELL).

Conference: Another name for a computer discussion group or mailing list. *See* List.

CPSR: Computer Professionals for Social Responsibility.

DPSWG: Digital Privacy and Security Working Group.

EES: Escrowed encryption standard.

EFF: Electronic Frontier Foundation.

Electronic mail: Messages sent via computer to the private electronic mailbox, or directory, of a person or organization. Usually called email.

Email: Electronic mail.

EPIC: Electronic Privacy Information Center.

File transfer protocol: *See* FTP.

Forum: On the WELL, a forum is a discussion list about a specific topic or sponsored by a specific group (such as, in the Lotus case, the Electronic Frontier Foundation). *Forum* is also a general term used to describe a newsgroup or list.

FTP: File transfer protocol. A protocol is a set of procedures that allow users to exchange data between computers. FTP is a specific protocol for transferring files from one computer to another and is part of the broader tcp/ip suite of protocols. *See also* Anonymous ftp.

Gopher: A menu-based system developed at the University of Minnesota for accessing sites across the Internet.

Header: The first part of an email message. Headers contain identifying information about a message, including addressee, sender, date, subject, and time.

Internet: A series of internetworked (interconnected) computers, which provide a backbone for connections worldwide. Computers connected to the Internet use the tcp/ip protocol suite and can provide email, file transfers, Usenet news, and telnet services.

List: An electronic mailing list, often using the listserv software, to which users post notes that are then distributed to the email boxes of all list members.

National Information Infrastructure (NII): The current name for the proposed "information superhighway," an upgraded version of the Internet that will employ fiber-optic technology and allow for transmission of text, sound, and visual data and will connect many networks and data providers.

Newsgroup: A bulletin board–like discussion group. *See* Usenet.

NII: *See* National Information Infrastructure.

NIST: National Institute for Standards and Technology.

NSA: National Security Agency.

Real-time chat: Synchronous computer-mediated communication, where users type in and read messages in real time.

RISKS Digest: A moderated mailing list, also available as a Usenet newsgroup (comp.risks), for discussions of "risks to the public in computers and related systems." This forum is supported by Committee on Computers and Public Policy of the Association for Computing Machinery (ACM).

Synchronous communication: Communications over computers in which data being sent and data being received are transferred with a predictable time relationship. Synchronous communications thus take place in real time. *See also* Asynchronous communication.

TCP/IP: Transmission control protocol/Internet protocol. A combination of many protocols, or sets of procedures, that allow data to be transferred over the Internet.

Telecom Digest: A moderated mailing list for discussions of telecommunications technologies.

Telecom Privacy Digest: A moderated mailing list, also available as a Usenet newsgroup (comp.privacy), for discussions of privacy issues related to telecommunications technologies.

Telnet: A protocol, or set of procedures, that allows users to log in to a remote computer. Telnet is part of the broader tcp/ip suite of protocols. *See also* Anonymous ftp, FTP.

Usenet: Similar to bulletin boards, Usenet is a system of newsgroups. Each newsgroup focuses on a specific topic and can be identified by its title. The newsgroup rec.cats, for example, is a recreational newsgroup about cats.

WELL: The Whole Earth 'Lectronic Link, a computer network based in Sausalito, California.

REFERENCES

Andrews, Edmund L. 1994. U.S. Plans to Push Giving F.B.I. Access in Computer Codes: "Clipper Chip" to Be Used. *New York Times*, February 5, A1, A48.

Aristotle. 1991. *On Rhetoric: A Theory of Civic Discourse*. Translated by George A. Kennedy. New York: Oxford University Press.

Avery Commercial Products Division. 1990. *Avery Joins Lotus to Make Label Printing Easy with New Lotus Marketplace*. Press release. Covina, Calif.: Avery Corporation.

Baker, John. 1991. Testimony. In *Domestic and International Data Protection Issues: Hearings before the Government Information, Justice, and Agriculture Subcommittee of the Committee on Government Operations House of Representatives*. April 10. Washington: GPO.

Barber, Benjamin R. 1984. *Strong Democracy: Participatory Politics for a New Age*. Berkeley: University of California Press.

Barton, Richard A. 1990. Testimony. In *Data Protection, Computers, and Changing Information Practices: Hearing before the Government Information, Justice, and Agriculture Subcommittee of the Committee on Government Operations House of Representatives*. May 10. Washington: GPO.

Baumlin, James S. 1994. Introduction: Positioning Ethos in Historical and Contemporary Theory. In *Ethos: New Essays in Rhetorical and Critical Theory*, edited by J. S. Baumlin and T. F. Baumlin. Dallas: Southern Methodist University Press.

Bennett, Colin J. 1992. *Regulating Privacy: Data Protection and Public Policy in Europe and the United States*. Ithaca: Cornell University Press.

Bitzer, Lloyd F. 1959. Aristotle's Enthymeme Revisited. *Quarterly Journal of Speech* 45: 399–408.

———. 1968. The Rhetorical Situation. *Philosophy and Rhetoric* 1: 1–14.

Bolter, Jay David. 1993. Hypertext and the Rhetorical Canons. In *Rhetorical Memory and Delivery*, edited by J. F. Reynolds. Hillsdale, N.J.: Erlbaum.

Bruffee, Kenneth A. 1986. "Social Construction, Language, and the Authority of Knowledge: A Bibliographic Essay." *College English* 48: 773–790.

Burke, Kenneth. 1969. *A Rhetoric of Motives*. Berkeley: University of California Press.

Burnham, David. 1980. *The Rise of the Computer State*. New York: Random House.

Carney, Eliza Newlin. 1993. Clashing over Clipper. *National Journal*, 25 (37): 2184–2187.

Cavazos, Edward A., and Gavino Morin. 1994. *Cyberspace and the Law: Your Rights and Duties in the On-Line World*. Cambridge: MIT Press.

Cherry, Roger D. 1988. Ethos versus Persona: Self-Representation in Written Discourse. *Written Communication* 5 (3): 251–276.

Cicero. 1970. *De Oratore*. Translated by J. S. Watson. Carbondale: Southern Illinois University Press.

Clark, Gregory. 1994. Rescuing the Discourse of Community. *College Composition and Communication* 45 (1): 61–74.

Cohen, Anthony P. 1985. *The Symbolic Construction of Community*. New York: Routledge.

Connors, Robert J. 1993. "Actio": A Rhetoric of Written Delivery (Iteration Two). In *Rhetorical Memory and Delivery*, edited by J. F. Reynolds. Hillsdale, N.J.: Erlbaum.

Covert, Colin. 1995. Cyberspace Remains a Masculine Environment. *Minneapolis Star Tribune*, A1, A10.

CPSR. 1993. NSA Seeks Delay in Clipper Case. Computer Professionals for Social Responsibility. August 15. Available from ftp.cpsr.org/cpsr/privacy/crypto/clipper/nsa__foia__delay__request.txt.

———. 1994. Electronic Petition to Oppose Clipper. Computer Professionals for Social Responsibility. January 31, 1994. Available from ftp . cpsr . org/cpsr/privacy/crypto/clipper/cpsr __ electronic__petition.txt.

Daly, James. 1994. Security Pros, Clinton Clash over Encryption Standards. *Computerworld,* January 31, 1994, 79.

Denning, Dorothy E. R. 1983. *Cryptography and Data Security.* Reading, Mass.: Addison-Wesley.

Deutsch, Linda (Associated Press). 1996. O. J. Tape Producer Threatens to Sue Those Who Block Orders. *St. Paul Pioneer Press,* January 12, 14A.

Doheny-Farina, Stephen. 1996. *The Wired Neighborhood.* New Haven: Yale University Press.

DPSWG. 1993. Letter to the President. Digital Privacy and Security Working Group. Available from ftp.eff.org.

Edelman, Lawrence. 1991. Chalk One Up for Privacy Rights. *Boston Globe,* January 24, 65–66.

Ellul, Jacques. 1964. *The Technological Society.* Translated by John Wilkinson. New York: Random House.

Equifax. 1991. *Equifax Discontinues Sale of Direct Marketing Lists Derived from Consumer Credit File.* Press release. Atlanta: Equifax.

Faigley, Lester. 1992. *Fragments of Rationality: Postmodernity and the Subject of Composition.* Pittsburgh: University of Pittsburgh Press.

Field, Anne R., Robert Neff, Frances Seghers, and Kathleen Deveny. 1987. "Big Brother Inc." May Be Closer Than You Thought. *Business Week,* February 9, 84–86.

Fisher, Lawrence M. 1991a. New Data Base Ended by Lotus and Equifax. *New York Times,* January 24, D4.

Fisher, Susan E. 1991b. What Do Computers Know about You? *PC Week,* February 11, 156–157.

Flaherty, David H. 1989. *Protecting Privacy in Surveillance Societies.* Chapel Hill: University of North Carolina Press.

Forbes, Malcolm S., Jr. 1994. High-Tech Snoops. *Forbes,* March 14, 26.

Former Lotus employee A. 1991. Electronic message to comp.society Usenet newsgroup.

———. 1993. Telephone interview with the author, March 1.

Former Lotus employee B. 1993. Telephone interview with the author, March 8.

Gates, Bill, Nathan Myhnold, and Peter Rinearson. 1995. *The Road Ahead*. New York: Viking.

Gibson, William. 1984. *Neuromancer*. New York: Ace.

Gurak, Laura J. 1996a. The Multi-Faceted and Novel Nature of Using Cyber-Texts as Research Data. In *Computer Networking and Scholarship in the Twenty-First Century*, edited by T. M. Harrison and T. D. Stephen. Albany: SUNY Press.

————. 1996b. Rhetorical Dynamics of Corporate Communication in Cyberspace: The Protest over Lotus MarketPlace. *IEEE Transactions on Professional Communication* 38 (1): 2–10.

Halloran, S. Michael. 1982. Aristotle's Concept of Ethos, or If Not His Somebody Else's. *Rhetoric Review* 1 (1): 58–63.

————. 1984. The Birth of Molecular Biology: An Essay in the Rhetorical Criticism of Scientific Discourse. *Rhetoric Review* 3 (1): 70–83.

Harasim, Linda M. 1993. Networlds: Networks as Social Space. In *Global Networks: Computers and International Communication*, edited by L. M. Harasim. Cambridge: MIT Press.

Harris, Joseph. 1989. The Idea of Community in the Study of Writing. *College Composition and Communication* 40 (1): 11–22.

Herring, Susan C. 1993. Gender and Democracy in Computer-Mediated Communication. *Electronic Journal of Communication* 3 (2): send email to Comserve@vm.its.rpi.edu with the command "Get Herring V3N293" (no quotation marks).

Hiltz, Starr Roxanne, and Murray Turoff. 1993. *The Network Nation: Human Communication via Computer*. Revised ed. Cambridge: MIT Press.

Hoffman, Lance J., ed. 1995. *Building in Big Brother: The Cryptographic Policy Debate*. New York: Springer-Verlag.

Hoke, Henry, Jr. 1990. Editorial. *Direct Marketing*, May, 96.

Hotz, Robert Lee. 1993. Computer Code's Security Worries Privacy Watchdogs. *Los Angeles Times*, October 4, A1, A20.

Johnson, Deborah G. 1985. *Computer Ethics*. Englewood Cliffs, N.J.: Prentice Hall.

Johnson, Nan. 1984. Ethos and the Aims of Rhetoric. In *Essays on Classical Rhetoric and Modern Discourse*, edited by R. J. Connors, L. S. Ede, and A. A. Lunsford. Carbondale: Southern Illinois University Press.

Kahn, David. 1972. *The Codebreakers*. New York: Macmillan.

Kantrowitz, Barbara. 1994. Men, Women, and Computers. *Newsweek*, May 16, 48–55.

Kaufer, David S., and Kathleen Carley. 1993. *Communication at a Distance: The Influence of Print on Sociocultural Organization and Change*. Hillsdale, N.J.: Erlbaum.

———. 1994. Some Concepts and Axioms about Communication: Proximate and at a Distance. *Written Communication* 11 (1): 8–42.

Kearney, Michael. 1995. Whiz Kid Anonymous: A Ten-Year-Old's Take on the Internet. *Utne Reader* 68 (March–April): 65.

Kramarae, Cheris, and Jana Kramer. 1995. Net Gains, Net Losses. *Women's Review of Books* 12 (5): 33–35.

Kramarae, Cheris, and H. Jeanie Taylor. 1993. Women and Men on Electronic Networks: A Conversation or a Monologue? In *Women, Information Technology, and Scholarship*, edited by H. J. Taylor, C. Kramarae, and M. Ebben. Urbana, Ill.: Center for Advanced Study.

Kuhn, Thomas S. 1970. *The Structure of Scientific Revolutions*. 3rd. ed. Chicago: University of Chicago Press.

Laclau, Ernesto. 1991. Community and Its Paradoxes: Richard Rorty's "Liberal Utopia." In *Community at Loose Ends*, edited by the Miami Theory Collective. Minneapolis: University of Minnesota Press.

Laudon, Kenneth C. 1986. *Dossier Society: Value Choices in the Design of National Information Systems*. New York: Columbia University Press.

Lea, Martin, Tim O'Shea, Pat Fung, and Russell Spears. 1992. "Flaming" in Computer-Mediated Communication: Observations, Explanations, Implications. In *Contexts of Computer-Mediated Communication*, edited by M. Lea. London: Harvester Wheatsheaf.

Lewis, Peter H. 1994. Of Privacy and Security: The Clipper Chip. *New York Times*, April 24, sec. 3, 5.

Licklider, J. R. C., R. W. Taylor, and E. Herbert. 1968. The Computer as a Communication Device. *Science and Technology* (April): 21–31.

Lotus Development Corporation. 1990. *Any Company Can Put Business Prospect Lists at Your Fingertips.* Brochure. Cambridge, Mass.: Lotus Development Corporation.

———. 1991. *Lotus, Equifax Cancel Shipment of Lotus MarketPlace: Households.* Press release. Cambridge, Mass.: Lotus Development Corporation.

Lyon, Arabella. 1992. Re-Presenting Communities: Teaching Turbulence. *Rhetoric Review* 10 (2): 279–290.

Markoff, John. 1993. Big Brother and the Computer Age. *New York Times*, May 6, D1, D7.

———. 1994a. Cyberspace under Lock and Key. *New York Times*, February 13, D4.

———. 1994b. U.S. Code Agency Is Jostling for Civilian Turf. *New York Times*, January 24, D1, D5.

———. 1995. Industry Rebuffs U.S. on Encryption. *New York Times*, November 8, C3.

Meador, Prentice A., Jr. 1983. Quintilian and the "Institutio Oratoria." In *A Synoptic History of Classical Rhetoric*, edited by J. J. Murphy. Davis, Calif.: Hermagoras.

Meeks, Brock N. 1995. Same Old Shit: The Government's Not-So-New "Clipper II": A Train Wreck Waiting to Happen. *Wired*, November, 88.

Miller, Carolyn R. 1993. Rhetoric and Community: The Problem of the One and the Many. In *Defining the New Rhetorics*, edited by Theresa Ends and Stuart C. Brown. Newbury Park, Calif.: Sage.

Mintz, John, and John Schwartz. 1993. Encryption Program Draws Fresh Attacks. *Washington Post*, September 18, C1, C6.

Mitchell, William J. 1995. *City of Bits: Space, Place, and the Infobahn.* Cambridge: MIT Press.

Morgan, Arthur E. 1942. *The Small Community: Foundation of Democratic Life.* New York: Harper and Brothers.

Mouffe, Chantal. 1991. Democratic Citizenship and the Political Community. In *Community at Loose Ends*, edited by the Miami Theory Collective. Minneapolis: University of Minnesota Press.

Negroponte, Nicholas. 1995. *Being Digital*. New York: Knopf.

NIST (National Institute of Standards and Technology). 1994. Approval of Federal Information Processing Standards Publication 185, Escrowed Encryption Standard (EES). *Federal Register* 59 (27): 5997–6005.

O'Connor, Rory J. 1991. Privacy Flap Kills Lotus Data Base. *San Jose Mercury News*, January 24, A1.

Odgen, Michael R. 1994. Politics in a Parallel Universe: Is There a Future for Cyberdemocracy? *Futures* 26 (7): 713–729.

Poplin, Dennis E. 1972. *Communities: A Survey of Theories and Methods of Research*. New York: Macmillan.

Porter, James E. 1992. *Audience and Rhetoric: An Archaeological Composition of the Discourse Community*. Englewood Cliffs, N.J.: Prentice Hall.

Quintilian, Marcus Fabius. *The Institutio Oratoria of Quintilian*, vol. 3. Translated by H. E. Butler. Cambridge: Harvard University Press.

Raymond, James C. 1984. Enthymemes, Examples, and Rhetorical Method. In *Essays on Classical Rhetoric and Modern Discourse*, edited by R. J. Connors, L. S. Ede, and A. A. Lunsford. Carbondale: Southern Illinois University Press.

Reynolds, Nedra. 1993. "Ethos" as Location: New Sites for Understanding Discursive Authority. *Rhetoric Review* 11 (2): 325–338.

Rheingold, Howard. 1993a. A Slice of Life in My Virtual Community. In *Global Networks: Computers and International Communication*, edited by L. M. Harasim. Cambridge: MIT Press.

———. 1993b. *The Virtual Community: Homesteading on the Electronic Frontier*. Reading, Mass.: Addison-Wesley.

Rice, Ronald E., and Gail Love. 1987. Electronic Emotion: Socio-Emotional Content in a Computer-Mediated Communication Network. *Communication Research* 14 (1): 85–105.

Rifkin, Jeremy. 1995. *The End of Work: The Decline of the Global*

Labor Force and the Dawn of the Post-Market Era. New York: Putnam.

Rotenberg, Marc. 1990. Testimony. In *Data Protection, Computers, and Changing Information Practices: Hearing before the Government Information, Justice, and Agriculture Subcommittee of the Committee on Government Operations House of Representatives.* May 16. Washington: GPO.

Rotenberg, Marc. 1992. Interview with the author. December 4.

―――. 1993a. Electronic mail message to the author. February 22.

―――. 1993b. Statement of CPSR Washington Office. In *Testimony before Department of Commerce, National Institute of Standards and Technology, Computer System Security and Privacy Advisory Board.* June 2. Washington: GPO.

Rothfeder, Jeffrey. 1989. Is Nothing Private? Computers Know More about You Than You Realize—and Now Anyone Can Tap In. *Business Week,* September 4, 74–82.

Rule, James. 1974. *Private Lives and Public Surveillance.* New York: Schocken.

Safire, William. 1994. Sink the Clipper Chip. *New York Times,* February 14, A17.

Salz, Rich. 1993. Electronic mail message to the author. February 9.

Schneier, Bruce. 1994. *Applied Cryptography.* New York: John Wiley and Sons.

Schwartz, John. 1993. U.S. Data Decoding Plan Delayed. *Washington Post,* June 8, A12.

Seiler, Larry. 1993. Electronic mail message to the author. February 12.

Selfe, Cynthia L., and Richard J. Selfe. 1996. Writing as Democratic Social Action in a Technological World: Politicizing and Inhabiting Virtual Landscapes. In *Nonacademic Writing: Social Theory and Technology,* edited by Ann Hill Duin and Craig Hansen. Mahwah, N.J.: Erlbaum.

Siegel, Jane, Vitaly Dubrovsky, Sara Kiesler, and Timothy W. McGuire. 1986. Group Processes in Computer-Mediated Communication. *Organizational Behavior and Human Decision Processes* 37: 157–187.

Smith, Ralph R., and Russel R. Windes. 1976. The Rhetoric of Mobilization: Implications for the Study of Movements. *Southern Speech Communication Journal* 42 (Fall 1976): 1–19.

Spears, Russell, and Martin Lea. 1994. Panacea or Panopticon?: The Hidden Power in Computer-Mediated Communication. *Communication Research* 21 (4): 427–459.

Spitzer, Michael. 1986. Writing Style in Computer Conferences. *IEEE Transactions on Professional Communication* 29 (1): 19–23.

Sproull, Lee, and Sara Kiesler. 1986. Reducing Social Context Cues: Electronic Mail in Organizational Communication. *Management Science* 32: 1492–512.

———. 1993. Computers, Networks, and Work. In *Global Networks: Computers and International Communication*, edited by L. M. Harasim. Cambridge: MIT Press.

Stoll, Clifford. 1995. *Silicon Snake Oil: Second Thoughts on the Information Highway*. New York: Doubleday.

Stone, Allucquere Rosanne. 1992. Will the Real Body Please Stand Up? Boundary Stories about Virtual Cultures. In *Cyberspace: First Steps*, edited by M. Benedikt. Cambridge: MIT Press.

Stowe, David W. 1995. Just Do It: How to Beat the Copyright Racket. *Lingua Franca* (November –December), 32–43.

Strangelove, Michael. 1994. The Internet as Catalyst for a Paradigm Shift. *Computer-Mediated Communication Magazine* (December).

Swales, John M. 1990. *Genre Analysis: English in Academic and Research Settings*. Cambridge: Oxford University Press.

Tannen, Deborah. 1990. *You Just Don't Understand: Women and Men in Conversation*. New York: Morrow.

Trubow, George B., ed. 1991. *Privacy Law and Practice*, vol. 3. New York: Matthew Bender.

Turkle, Sherry. 1995. *Life on the Screen: Identity in the Age of the Internet*. New York: Simon and Schuster.

Vatz, Richard E. 1973. The Myth of the Rhetorical Situation. *Philosophy and Rhetoric* 6: 154–161.

Von Rospach, Chug. 1994. A Primer on How to Work with the Usenet Community. Available on various Usenet newsgroups, including news.misc and news.answers. Archive name usenet-primer/part1.

Walker, Jeffrey. 1994. The Body of Persuasion: A Theory of the Enthymeme. *College English* 56 (1): 46–65.

Walls, Jan. 1993. Global Networking for Local Development: Task Focus and Relationship Focus in Cross-Cultural Communication. In *Global Networks: Computers and International Communication*, edited by L. M. Harasim. Cambridge: MIT Press.

Weizenbaum, Joseph. 1976. *Computer Power and Human Reason: From Judgement to Calculation.* San Francisco: Freeman.

Welch, Kathleen E. 1990. Electrifying Classical Rhetoric: Ancient Media, Modern Technology, and Contemporary Composition. *Journal of Advanced Composition* 10 (1): 22–38.

Werry, Chris. 1993. The Rhetoric of Interactive Written Discourse. Paper presented at Penn State Conference on Rhetoric and Composition, State College, Penn.

Westin, Alan F., and Michael A. Baker. 1972. *Databanks in a Free Society.* New York: Quadrangle.

White House. 1993. Statement by the Press Secretary. April 16. Washington, D.C.: Office of the Press Secretary.

Wilke, John R. 1990. Lotus Product Spurs Fears about Privacy. *Wall Street Journal*, November 13, B1, B5.

Winner, Langdon. 1991. A Victory for Computer Populism. *Technology Review* (May–June): 66.

Zuboff, Shoshana. 1988. *In the Age of the Smart Machine.* New York: Basic Books.

———. 1995. The Emperor's New Workplace. *Scientific American* (September): 202–204.